WOODLAND
KNITS

WOODLAND KNITS

Over 20 enchanting patterns

A Tiny Owl Knits Collection
by Stephanie Dosen

PHOTOGRAPHY BY TIFFANY MUMFORD

The Taunton Press

The Taunton Press
Inspiration for hands-on living®

Published in the United States by
The Taunton Press, 63 S. Main Street,
PO Box 5506, Newtown CT 06470-5506
email: tp@taunton.com

Publishing Director Jane O'Shea
Creative Director Helen Lewis
Commissioning Editor Lisa Pendreigh
Pattern Checker Sally Harding
Designer Gemma Wilson
Photographer Tiffany Mumford
Hair and Make Up Artist Carolyn Wren
Stylist Anna Woodham
Models Natalee May, Natanya Louise
Waybourne, Charlotte 'Crumpet' Gwynn
and Stephanie Dosen
Production Director Vincent Smith
Production Controller Aysun Hughes

Library of Congress Cataloging-in-Publication Data
in progress

ISBN: 978-1-62710-024-3

Printed in China

10 9 8 7 6 5 4 3 2 1
First American Edition

Originally published in the
United Kingdom by
Quadrille Publishing Ltd.,
London, in 2013.

CONTENTS

INTRODUCTION

Hello my lovelies. I'm so happy you are here in the magical forest with me!

Welcome to my very first Tiny Owl Knits collection entitled *Woodland Knits*. You must be reading this because we share the same sense of woodland wonder about the enchanted forest. I'd even bet that you dream about the mysterious little creatures that live there —seen and unseen—and want to work a little of their style into your own. I feel the very same way!

I was inspired by faerie tales and the spirit of the woodland when I was creating these designs to share with you. Now I can't say for certain that I've ever seen a gnome or a faerie knitting, but I'm sure they do it curled up by their fireplaces just the same as we do. So grab some needles and enjoy your journey through the trees with me as the forest brings just a touch of magic to our everyday knitting.

Happy knits!

Love,
Stephanie *xoxo*
Tiny Owl Knits

KNITTING TIPS FOR OWLIES

Here are some special knitting tips for you to read before you start your woodland knits. Along with these tips, the Tiny Owl Stitch Dictionary opposite has explanations for the abbreviations used in the instructions. Many knitters will already know these by heart, but it's always good to have them at hand just in case you need a reminder.

OWL EXPERIENCE LEVELS

When choosing a design to knit, have a look at the skill level marked at the beginning of the pattern. It is a rough guide to how easy or difficult the knitting will be:

 suitable for beginner knitters

suitable for intermediate knitters

suitable for experienced knitters

Pick a one-owl design if you want a relaxing knit, a two-owl for something with a few more enticing details, or a three-owl for more challenging and intricate knitting. An absolute beginner knitter can start with something easy like the Bo Peep Scarf on pages 22–25 to gain knitting confidence, and jump right into the two-owl knits after that.

CHOOSING NEEDLES AND YARNS

Always use your favorite type of knitting needles, whether metal or bamboo, as this will make the process so much more enjoyable. Good quality needles are definitely worth paying a little extra for—remember, they will last you a lifetime.

The yarns I used are listed at the beginning of each knitting pattern. Detailed information for the yarns is given on pages 126 and 127. You can use a substitute yarn, but be sure to take into account the feel, color, and quality of the yarn you choose. Don't rush when deciding on a substitute yarn; it's worth taking the time to find the perfect one.

GAUGE SWATCHES

The gauge given in each knitting pattern is the gauge I used for that particular design. To achieve the same gauge, you may have to use a different size needle so be sure to make a gauge swatch before you begin. Working to an exact gauge is not always that important—say for a scarf or bag—but if you can match the gauge your pieces of knitting will come out the same size as mine and match the specified dimensions.

COUNTING STITCHES

Stitch counts (in *italic*) are given at the end of a row or a section in a knitting pattern after the stitches on your needle have been increased or decreased. Count your stitches whenever you come to a stitch count to ensure that you have the correct number of stitches on your needle.

Did you know there is a parliament of friendly owls on the tiny owl knits message board? We have lots of fun hooting and hollering so pop by if you have a question or just need a pick-me-up chat!
www.ravelry.com/groups/ tiny-owl-knits

TINY OWL STITCH DICTIONARY

These are the general abbreviations used in this book—they make your patterns easier (and quicker!) to follow. Any special abbreviations are given with the individual patterns.

beg	begin(ning)	**rem**	remain(s)(ing)
CC	contrasting color	**rep**	repeat(ing)
ch	chain (crochet term)	**RS**	right side
cm	centimeter(s)	**sc**	single crochet (crochet term)
cont	continu(e)(ing)	**sl**	slip
dc	double crochet (crochet term)	**sl st**	slip stitch (crochet term)
dec	decreas(e)(ing)	**ssk**	slip next two stitches one at a time
DK	double-knitting yarn		knitwise onto right needle, insert left
	(a lightweight yarn)		needle purlwise into front of two slipped
dpn(s)	double-pointed knitting needle(s)		stitches and knit them together
g	gram(s)	**St st**	stockinette stitch (knit one row,
in	inch(es)		purl one row)
inc 1	knit into front and back of stitch	**st(s)**	stitch(es)
k	knit	**WS**	wrong side
k2tog	knit the next two stitches together	**yd**	yard(s)
m	meter(s)	**yo**	take yarn from front to back over
m1	lift up strand between stitch just		right needle to make a new stitch
	worked and next stitch with tip of		
	left needle (front to		
	back) and knit into		
	back of lifted stitch		
MC	main color		
mm	millimeter(s)		
p	purl		
p2tog	purl the next two		
	stitches together		
psso	pass slipped		
	stitch over		

DEER WITH LITTLE ANTLERS HAT

Are you tired of trying to grow antlers with no luck? Then this little hat is for you. It is perfect to wear when hanging out with your animal friends in the woods. You will blend in like a charm.

OWL EXPERIENCE LEVEL

SIZES

	ADULT	CHILD
To fit head circumference	22"	19"
	56cm	48cm
Hat width (measured flat	9½"	8½"
across ribbed edge)	24cm	21.5cm

Note: The instructions for the child's size, where they differ from the adult size, are given in parentheses ( ).

YOU WILL NEED

* **MC** 1 × 100g hank of an aran-weight wool yarn (4), such as Manos del Uruguay *Wool Clasica* (138yd/126m per hank; 100% wool) in mid brown (I Quail)
* **CC1** 1 × 50g ball of a double-knitting-weight wool tweed yarn (3), such as Rowan *Tweed* (129yd/118m per ball; 100% wool) in off-white (580 Arncliffe), for antlers
  Be sure to use wool yarn that felts!
* **CC2** 1 × 50g ball of a fingering-weight wool yarn (1), such as Rowan *Pure Wool 4-ply* (174yd/160m per ball; 100% superwash wool) in pale pink (449 Vintage), for inner ears

* US size 10½ (6.5mm) circular knitting needle, 16" (40cm) long
* Set of US size 10½ (6.5mm) double-pointed knitting needles (dpns)
* Pair of US size 5 (3.75mm) knitting needles, for inner ears
* Set of US size 9 (5.5mm) double-pointed knitting needles (dpns), for antlers
* Off-white sewing thread, for sewing on antlers
* Stitch markers and blunt-ended yarn needle

GAUGE

14 sts and 18 rows to 4" (10cm) square measured over St st using US size 10½ (6.5mm) needles and MC. *Use needle size needed to obtain correct gauge.*
Note: Don't be afraid to go up a needle size to achieve the correct gauge as MC (an aran-weight wool yarn) is knitted loosely to achieve the right texture for the hat.

DEER WITH LITTLE ANTLERS HAT

Ready? Let's go!

TINY OWL STITCH DICTIONARY

See page 9 for general knitting abbreviations.

TO MAKE THE HAT

Using US size 10½ (6.5mm) circular needle and MC, cast on 64 (56) sts. Place a stitch marker at beg of round and join in the round. (Slip marker when it is reached at beg of each round.)

Rib round: *K1, p1; rep from * to end of round. Repeat rib round 3 times more.

Change to St st (knit every round) and work until hat measures 5½"/14cm (4½"/11.5cm) from cast-on edge.

Shape top of hat

Note: When shaping the hat change to US size 10½ (6.5mm) double-pointed needles when necessary, as hat gets too small for the circular needle.

Beg shaping as follows:

Round 1 and all-odd numbered rounds: Knit.

Round 2: *K6, k2tog; rep from * to end. *56 (49) sts.*

Round 4: *K5, k2tog; rep from * to end. *48 (42) sts.*

Round 6: *K4, k2tog; rep from * to end. *40 (35) sts.*

Round 8: *K3, k2tog; rep from * to end. *32 (28) sts.*

Round 10: *K2, k2tog; rep from * to end. *24 (21) sts.*

Round 12: *K1, k2tog; rep from * to end. *16 (14) sts.*

Round 14: *K2tog; rep from * to end. *8 (7) sts.*

Cut off yarn, leaving a long yarn tail.

Using a blunt-ended yarn needle, thread yarn tail through rem 8 (7) live sts, cinching them closed.

YARN AND PATTERN NOTES

A pink fingering yarn in any fiber for the inside of the ears will work and you don't need much (I held it with a strand of pink Rowan *Kidsilk Haze* mohair to give it fuzziness). You knit the ears separately in the round, then sew them to the hat. The antlers are also made separately, but are then felted (p. 14) before they are attached. You don't need much yarn for the antlers either. Any double-knitting-weight off-white 100% felting wool will work. Remember, very white wool will not felt because it has been overly bleached. Try to find a natural-looking "white" or cream, as they are often not processed so much. Do a little felting test before you start.

TO MAKE THE EARS (MAKE 2)

Using US size 10½ (6.5mm) dpns and MC, cast on 20 (16) sts (leaving a long loose yarn end) and divide the sts evenly over three dpns (you knit with the 4th dpn). Place a stitch marker at beg of round and join in the round. (Slip marker when it is reached at beg of each round.)

Knit 10 (8) rounds.

Shape top of ear

Adult size only (for child size, skip to round 14)

Round 11: K3, k2tog, ssk, k6, k2tog, ssk, k3. *16 (–) sts.*

Rounds 12 and 13: Knit.

Both sizes

Round 14: K2, k2tog, ssk, k4, k2tog, ssk, k2. *12 sts.*

Round 15: Knit.

Round 16: K1, k2tog, ssk, k2, k2tog, ssk, k1. *8 sts.*

Round 17: Knit.

Round 18: [K2tog, ssk] twice. *4 sts.*

Q. HOW DO I FELT THE ANTLERS?

A. Easy! Wet the antlers with some hot water, squirt a dab of hand soap on your palms (try lavender or patchouli scented soap—yum!) and "wash your hands with the antlers in the middle." After about 4 or 5 minutes watch them magically shrink. (Not your hands, the antlers.) When the antlers look pretty well felted, spend a good amount of time pinching, rolling, and sculpting the fibers to get the antlers to curl in at the tips and the bottoms to open out with a slight flare at the base. They will dry in the shape you leave them so sculpting them is a crucial step. I spent more time molding them than I did knitting and felting them. Felting tip—less is more when it comes to soap and water. Agitation is the key. Don't give up!

Q. DO I HAVE TO FELT THE ANTLERS?

A. Nope! Lots of people have opted out of felting the antlers.

Round 19: [K2tog] twice, pass first st on right needle over second st and off needle.
Cut yarn and fasten off.

TO MAKE THE PINK INNER EARS (MAKE 2)

For both sizes, follow these same instructions.
Using US size 5 (3.75mm) needles and CC2, cast on 7 sts.
Row 1 and all odd-numbered rows: Purl.
Row 2 (RS): Knit.
Row 4: Knit.
Row 6: Ssk, k3, k2tog. *5 sts.*
Row 8: Ssk, k1, k2tog. *3 sts.*
Row 10: Slip 1 st knitwise, k2tog, pass slipped st over 2nd st on right needle and off needle.
Cut off yarn and fasten off.
Aligning the cast-on edges, sew the pink ear to the middle of the big ear using a simple running stitch. Fold the cast-on edge of the big ear in half like a taco and sew together along the cast-on edge.

TO MAKE THE ANTLERS (MAKE 2)

The antlers are the same for both sizes.
Using US size 9 (5.5mm) dpns and CC1, cast on 8 sts and divide sts evenly over two dpns (you knit with a 3rd dpn). Join in the round.
Knit 6 rounds.
Round 7: K4, [k2tog] twice. *6 sts.*
Knit 5 rounds.
Round 13: Ssk, k2, k2tog. *4 sts.*
Round 14: Knit.
Round 15: [Ssk] twice, pass first st on right needle over second st and off needle.
Cut off yarn and fasten off. Weave in yarn end.
Prong 1
Lay the antler flat with the tail off to the right. Count 8 rows up from the cast-on edge along the left side of the antler, and using a US size 9 (5.5mm) dpn and CC1, join yarn and pick up and knit 4 sts along edge, working toward the base (cast-on edge) of the antler.

Using two dpns, now work I-cord as follows:
Round 1: Knit, do not turn work.
Round 2: With same side of work still facing, slide sts to other end of dpn, take yarn around back of sts, pull yarn tight and knit sts again, do not turn work.
Rounds 3, 4, and 5: Rep round 2.
Round 6: With same side still facing, slide sts to other end of dpn, take yarn around back of sts, pull yarn tight and [ssk] twice, pass first st on right needle over second st and off needle.
Cut off yarn and fasten off.
Prong 2
Count 3 rows up from beg of prong 1, and using a US size 9 (5.5mm) dpn and CC1, join yarn and pick up and knit 2 sts along the left side of the antler.
Using two dpns, work 3 rounds of I-cord as before.
Round 4: With same side of work still facing, pass first st on right needle over second st and off needle.
Cut off yarn and fasten off. Leave the yarn tails on the antlers and trim them after felting. ***
OK, now felt the antlers! Don't be alarmed if your antlers look less than perfect after they are freshly felted—simply mold them into shape.
Whipstitch the ears and the antlers to the hat around their bases, using matching yarn for the ears and off-white sewing thread for the antlers. Use the photograph opposite for placement.
Naw, mine's not perfect!

I hope you will love your deery hat! Wear your antlers with pride.

MOONBEAM DUSTER

Cowboys in the old West wore dusters to keep their jeans
dust-free. If you ever roam the forest during a full moon,
you are going to get full of moon-dust! This moonbeam duster
will do its best to keep your petticoats clean and tidy.

OWL EXPERIENCE LEVEL

SIZES	XS	S	M	L	XL	XXL
To fit bust	28–30"	32–34"	36–38"	40–42"	44–46"	48–50"
	71–76cm	81–86cm	91–96cm	101–106cm	112–117cm	122–127cm
Duster around bust	23¼"	27¼"	30¾"	34¼"	38¼"	41¾"
	59cm	68cm	77cm	86cm	94cm	105cm

YOU WILL NEED

* **MC** 1 (1: 2: 2: 3: 3) × 100g hanks of a
  heavy-worsted-weight wool yarn , such
  as Malabrigo *Merino Worsted* (210yd/192m
  per hank; 100% merino wool) in pale lilac
  (36 Pearl)
* **CC** A total of approximately 546 (637: 715:
  806: 884: 975)yd/504 (588: 660: 744: 816:
  900)m of an assortment of complementary
  fingering-weight to worsted-weight yarns
  for the fringe. For the curious, I used the
  following yarns:
* Brooklyn Tweed *Loft* in green (02 Tent)
* Classic Elite *La Gran* mohair in dusty green-
  blue (6595 Porcelain Blue)
* Jamieson's of Shetland *Spindrift* in gold
  (429 Old Gold), pale blue (769 Willow),
  light mauve (562 Cyclamen), and purple
  mélange (1270 Purple Haze)
* Knit Picks *Palette* in dark gold (25100
  Serpentine), light blue-violet (24012 Iris
  Heather), pale mauve (26037 Seraphim),
  and olive green (25545 Caper)
* Koigu *KPPPM* in a speckled natural, and in
  three solid colors—violet, purple-gray, and
  pale blue
* Plymouth *Encore Worsted* in earthy heather
  brown (1405 Light Walnut Mix) and pale
  dusty green (801 Light Colonial Green)
* Rowan *Felted Tweed* in beige (157 Camel)
* Rowan *Fine Tweed* in earthy tan (378 Litton)
* Rowan *Kidsilk Haze* mohair in plum (600
  Dewberry), pale dusty lilac (589 Majestic),
  and pale green-blue (581 Meadow)
* Pair of US size 10½ (6.5mm) knitting
  needles
* Crochet hook, for attaching the fringe
* Blunt-ended yarn needle

Ready? Let's go!

GAUGE

14 sts and 21 rows to 4" (10cm) square measured over St st using US size 10½ (6.5mm) needles and MC. *Use needle size needed to obtain correct gauge.* Note: The MC yarn normally calls for a smaller needle size. I've gone up in needle size for a looser fabric.

TINY OWL STITCH DICTIONARY

See page 9 for general knitting abbreviations.

YARN AND PATTERN NOTES

This is a great project for scraps or mini-skeins! The body of the vest is knitted flat in three pieces and the fun duster fringe is added afterward. Choosing fringe yarns from your scraps is the fun part. Don't feel limited to use what I've used—that would be expensive!

TO MAKE THE BACK

Using US size 10½ (6.5mm) needles and MC, cast on 52 (59: 66: 73: 80: 87) sts.
Row 1 (WS): Purl.
Row 2 (RS): Knit.
[Repeat rows 1 and 2] 6 (6: 6: 8: 8: 10) times more, so ending with a RS row—a total of *14 (14: 14: 18: 18: 22) rows* have been worked from cast-on edge.
Shape armholes
Row 1 (WS): Bind off 3 sts, purl to end.
Row 2 (RS): Bind off 3 sts, knit to end. *46 (53: 60: 67: 74: 81) sts.*
Row 3: Slip 1 st purlwise, k1, p1, k1, purl to last 4 sts, [k1, p1] twice.
Row 4: Ssk, p1, k1, p1, knit to last 5 sts, p1, k1, p1, k2tog.
[Repeat rows 3 and 4] 5 times more, so ending with a RS row. *34 (41: 48: 55: 62: 69) sts.*
Now stop decreases and work as follows:
Row 1 (WS): [P1, k1] twice, purl to last 4 sts, [k1, p1] twice.
Row 2 (RS): [P1, k1] twice, knit to last 4 sts, [k1, p1] twice.
Row 3: [K1, p1] twice, purl to last 4 sts, [p1, k1] twice.
Row 4: [K1, p1] twice, knit to last 4 sts, [p1, k1] twice.
Repeat rows 1–4 until armhole measures 9 (9: 9: 9½: 10: 10½)"/23 (23: 23: 24: 25.5: 26.5)cm, ending with a WS row.
Bind off in pattern.

TO MAKE THE RIGHT FRONT

Using US size 10½ (6.5mm) needles and MC, cast on 18 (21: 24: 27: 30: 33) sts.

Row 1 (WS): Purl to last 4 sts, [p1, k1] twice.

Row 2 (RS): [P1, k1] twice, knit to end.

Row 3: Purl to last 4 sts, [k1, p1] twice.

Row 4: [K1, p1] twice, knit to end.

[Repeat rows 1–4] 2 (2: 3: 3: 4: 4) times more. Repeat rows 1 and 2 once more, so ending with a RS row—a total of *14 (14: 18: 18: 22: 22) rows* have been worked from cast-on edge.

Shape armholes

Row 1 (WS): Bind off 3 sts, k1, p1, k1, purl to last 4 sts, [k1, p1] twice. *15 (18: 21: 24: 27: 30) sts.*

Row 2 (RS): [K1, p1] twice, knit to last 4 sts, [p1, k1] twice.

Row 3 (WS): P2tog, k1, p1, k1, purl to last 4 sts, [p1, k1] twice.

Row 4: [P1, k1] twice, knit to last 4 sts, [p1, k1] twice.

Row 5: P2tog, k1, p1, k1, purl to last 4 sts, [k1, p1] twice.

Rows 6–13: Rep rows 2–5 twice. *9 (12: 15: 18: 21: 24) sts.*

Size XS only

Row 14 (RS): [K1, p1] 3 times, k1, p2tog. *8 sts.*

Rows 15 and 16: [P1, k1] 4 times.

Rows 17 and 18: [K1, p1] 4 times.

Repeat rows 15–18 until armhole measures 9"/23cm.

Bind off in pattern.

Sizes S, M, L, XL, and XXL only

Row 14 (RS): [K1, p1] twice, knit to last 5 sts, k1, p1, k1, p2tog. *–(11: 14: 17: 20: 23) sts.*

Row 15: [P1, k1] twice, purl to last 4 sts, [p1, k1] twice.

Row 16: [P1, k1] twice, knit to last 4 sts, [p1, k1] twice.

Row 17: [K1, p1] twice, purl to last 4 sts, [k1, p1] twice.

Row 18: [K1, p1] twice, knit to last 4 sts, [k1, p1] twice.

Repeat rows 15–18 until armhole measures –(9: 9½: 10: 10½: 11)"/–(23: 24: 25.5: 26.5: 28)cm. Bind off in pattern.

TO MAKE THE LEFT FRONT

Using US size 10½ (6.5mm) needles and MC, cast on 18 (21: 24: 27: 30: 33) sts.

Row 1 (WS): [K1, p1] twice, purl to end.

Row 2 (RS): Knit to last 4 sts, [k1, p1] twice.

Row 3: [P1, k1] twice, purl to end.

Row 4: Knit to last 4 sts, [p1, k1] twice.

[Repeat rows 1–4] 2 (2: 3: 3: 4: 4) times more. Repeat rows 1–3 once more, so ending with a WS row—a total of *15 (15: 19: 19: 23: 23) rows* have been worked from cast-on edge.

Shape armholes

Row 1 (RS): Bind off 3 sts, knit to last 4 sts, [p1, k1] twice. *15 (18: 21: 24: 27: 30) sts.*

Row 2 (WS): [K1, p1] twice, purl to last 5 sts, k1, p1, k1, p2tog.

Row 3: [K1, p1] twice, knit to last 4 sts, [k1, p1] twice.

Row 4: [P1, k1] twice, purl to last 5 sts, k1, p1, k1, p2tog.

Row 5: [K1, p1] twice, knit to last 4 sts, [p1, k1] twice.

Rows 6–13: Rep rows 2–5 twice. *9 (12: 15: 18: 21: 24) sts.*

Size XS only

Row 14 (WS): [K1, p1] 3 times, k1, p2tog. *8 sts.*

Row 15: [K1, p1] 4 times.

Rows 16 and 17: [P1, k1] 4 times.

Row 18: [K1, p1] 4 times.

Repeat rows 15–18 until armhole measures 9"/23cm.

Bind off in pattern.

Sizes S, M, L, XL, and XXL only

Row 14 (WS): [K1, p1] twice, purl to last 5 sts, k1, p1, k1, p2tog. *–(11: 14: 17: 20: 23) sts.*

Row 15: [K1, p1] twice, knit to last 4 sts, [k1, p1] twice.

Row 16: [P1, k1] twice, purl to last 4 sts, [p1, k1] twice.

Row 17: [P1, k1] twice, knit to last 4 sts, [p1, k1] twice.

Row 18: [K1, p1] twice, purl to last 4 sts, [k1, p1] twice.

Repeat rows 15–18 until armhole measures –(9: 9½: 10: 10½: 11)"/–(23: 24: 25.5: 26.5: 28)cm. Bind off in pattern.

TO SEW THE SEAMS

Weave in all yarn ends. Using mattress stitch, sew the right front to the back along the sides making sure the armholes line up. Then sew the bound-off edge of the right front to the bound-off edge of the back right shoulder. Sew on the left front in the same way.

TO ADD THE FRINGE

The fringe consists of approximately 42 (49: 55: 62: 68: 75) fringe clumps, each 22" (56cm) long. Each fringe clump uses about 13yd (12m) of yarn.

Cut ten 46" (117cm) strands of CC yarn per clump, then fold the ten strands in half to make 20 strands.

Attach the fringe clumps to approximately every other stitch along the bottom (cast-on edge) of the duster using a crochet hook. On the wrong side, insert the crochet hook from front to back through the cast-on stitch and through the loop at the folded end of the fringe clump. Pull the clump loop through the stitch. Now pull the strands of yarn through the loop and tighten. Trim any uneven strands from each clump to make sure the edges are all nice and straight.

Don your duster and you are ready for a moonlit walk in the forest. No fear of moon-dust now!

HELPFUL TIP

Make your clumps artfully, so that each one is a little bit different but they work well together. It will keep it interesting to the eye if you don't use all of the same colors in every single fringe clump. Have fun and experiment!

BO PEEP SCARF

Oh, I hope you will love wearing your Bo Peep Scarf as much as I love wearing mine. It has the fuzzy power to cheer up a drab day in a bunny-loving minute. Wear it when tending your sheep, or when making a "present"-ation at work. Get it? Cause you kinda look like a present. He he he. Sorry. Had to.

OWL EXPERIENCE LEVEL

SIZE

One size to fit 12½" (32cm) neck, but the scarf is easily adjustable
Scarf length, measured flat from point to point, is 62" (157.5cm)

YOU WILL NEED

* **MC1** 1 × 100g hank of a fingering-weight alpaca yarn (**1**), such as Blue Sky Alpacas *Royal* (288yd/263m per hank; 100% royal alpaca) in pale cameo pink (704 Cameo)
* **MC2** 1 × 25g ball of a fine-weight mohair/silk yarn (**2**), such as Rowan *Kidsilk Haze* (229yd/210m per ball; 70% super kid mohair, 30% silk) in pale pink (580 Grace)

* Pair of US size 3 (3mm) knitting needles, 10" (25cm) long
* Safety pin and blunt-ended yarn needle

GAUGE

24 sts to 4" (10cm) measured over St st using US size 3 (3mm) needles and one strand of MC1 and one strand of MC2 held together. *Use needle size needed to obtain correct gauge.*

TINY OWL STITCH DICTIONARY

See page 9 for general knitting abbreviations.

Ready? Let's go!

TO MAKE THE SCARF

Using US size 3 (3mm) and one strand each of MC1 and MC2 held together throughout, cast on 25 sts.

Row 1 (RS): Inc 1, k to last 5 sts, ssk, k3.
Row 2: K5, p to last 5 sts, k5.
Repeat last 2 rows until work measures 6" (15cm) from beg, ending with a WS row.
Note: If you need more neck room, this is the place to conserve yarn by working less than 6" (15cm).
Row 1 (RS): K3, k2tog, k to last 5 sts, ssk, k3.
Row 2: K5, p to last 5 sts, k5.
Repeat last 2 rows until 11 sts remain, ending with a WS row.
**Row 1 (RS): Inc 1, k to last 2 sts, inc 1, k1.
Row 2: K5, p to last 5 sts, k5.
Repeat last 2 rows until you have 39 sts, ending with a WS row.
Row 1 (RS): Knit.
Row 2: K5, p to last 5 sts, k5.
Row 3: Inc 1, k to last 2 sts, inc 1, k1.
Row 4: K5, p to last 5 sts, k5.
Repeat last 4 rows until there are 45 sts, ending with a row 4.
Mark end of last row to help you measure the next section, using a safety pin or a colored thread as your marker.
Row 1 (RS): Knit.
Row 2: K5, p to last 5 sts, k5.
Repeat last 2 rows until work measures 4" (10cm) from marker, ending with a WS row.
Row 1 (RS): K3, k2tog, k to last 5 sts, ssk, k3.
Row 2: K5, p to last 5 sts, k5.
Row 3: Knit.
Row 4: K5, p to last 5 sts, k5.
Repeat last 4 rows until there are 39 sts, ending with a row 4.***

Row 1 (RS): K3, k2tog, k to last 5 sts, ssk, k3.
Row 2: K5, p to last 5 sts, k5.
Repeat last 2 rows until there are 21 sts, ending with a WS row.
Mark end of last row.
Row 1 (RS): Knit.
Row 2: K5, p to last 5 sts, k5.
Repeat last 2 rows until work measures 18" (45.5cm) from last marker or the circumference of your neck plus another 5½" (14cm), ending with a WS row.

Ready for the other side of the bow?
Good, me too!

Go back and repeat from ** to ***.
*Don't forget to STOP at *** this time though.*
Then cont from here as follows:
Row 1 (RS): K3, k2tog, k to last 5 sts, ssk, k3.
Row 2: K5, p to last 5 sts, k5.
Repeat last 2 rows until 11 sts remain, ending with a WS row.
Row 1 (RS): Inc 1, k to last 2 sts, inc 1, k1.
Row 2: K5, p to last 5 sts, k5.
Repeat last 2 rows until there are 25 sts, ending with a WS row.
Mark end of last row.

Row 1 (RS): K3, k2tog, k to last 2 sts, inc 1, k1.
Row 2: K5, p to last 5 sts, k5.
Repeat last 2 rows until work measures 6" (15cm) from last marker—or for desired length if you adjusted it at the beginning—ending with a WS row.
Bind off.
Weave in yarn ends securely.
YAY! It's finished.

Voila! You are wrapped up like a cute present! Take extra care when sitting under pine trees that little children don't accidentally try to unwrap you.

Q. HOW DO I WEAR THIS THING!?

A. Easy! Simply tie it just like you would tie your shoelaces, or a Christmas bow. Put it around your neck pretty side (right side) out, and first make the little crossy bit (don't make a double knot though), then make the bow. Take extra time and care to make sure that the RS of the stockinette stitch is showing for the bow petals. This may take some twisting and arranging to get it to look like a perfect bow. (Just like when you make a bow in real life with ribbon, it takes a minute to get it just right.) The garter-stitch edging curls under to make a nice edge.

TINY VIOLET HAND PUFF

Shy violets decorate this little hand puff, perfect for forest spring walking. And so soft and cozy for winter walks, too.

OWL EXPERIENCE LEVEL

SIZE

10" (25.5cm) wide by 7" (18cm) high

YOU WILL NEED

* **MC** 1 × 100g ball of a super-bulky-weight wool yarn (6), such as Rowan *Big Wool* (87yd/80m per ball; 100% merino wool) in ecru (048 Linen), for base
* **A** 1 × 50g ball of an aran-weight angora yarn (4), such as Naturally *Sensation* (131yd/120m per ball; 70% merino wool, 30% angora) in white, for lining—use two strands held together
* **B** 2 × 50g hanks of a sport-weight alpaca yarn (2), such as Blue Sky Alpacas *Sport Weight* (110yd/100m per hank; 100% alpaca) in dark purple (512 Eggplant), for violets
* **C** 2 × 50g hanks of a sport-weight alpaca yarn (2), such as Blue Sky Alpacas *Sport Weight* (110yd/100m per hank; 100% alpaca) in violet-blue (523 Grape), for violets
* **D** 1 × 50g hank of a sport-weight alpaca yarn (2), such as Blue Sky Alpacas *Melange* (110yd/100m per hank; 100% alpaca) in mustard (807 Dijon), for stamens
* **E** 1 × 100g ball of a super-bulky-weight wool yarn (6), such as Rowan *Big Wool* (87yd/80m per ball; 100% merino wool) in dark green (043 Forest), for leaves and vines
* US size size 13 (9mm) circular knitting needle, 16" (40cm) long
* US size 10 (6mm) circular knitting needle, 16" (40cm) long
* Spare US size 10 (6mm) or smaller circular knitting needle, 16" (40cm) long, for holding sts while grafting seam
* US size I/9 (5.5mm) crochet hook
* US size G/6 (4mm) crochet hook
* 1½yd (1.5m) of green velvet ribbon, 1¼" (3cm) wide, for optional strap
* Stitch marker and blunt-ended yarn needle

GAUGE

10 sts to 4" (10cm) measured over St st using US size 13 (9mm) needles and MC. *Use needle size needed to obtain correct gauge.*

TINY OWL STITCH DICTIONARY

See page 9 for general knitting abbreviations.

Ready? Let's go!

TO MAKE THE PUFF BASE WITH LINING

The puff base and lining are made in one piece—a long tube.

Puff base

Using US size 10 (6mm) circular needle and MC, cast on 24 sts, using an open or provisional cast-on method. Place a stitch marker at beg of round and join in the round. (Slip marker when it is reached at beg of each round.)

Knit 2 rounds.

Yes, it's tight, but that's OK—keep going.

Next round (inc round): *K1, inc 1; rep from * to end of round. *36 sts.*

Change to US size 13 (9mm) circular needle and cont to knit every round until work measures 7" (18cm) from beg of MC at cast-on edge.

Change back to US size 10 (6mm) needle.

Next round (dec round): *K1, k2tog; rep from * to end of round. *24 sts.*

Knit 2 rounds.

Lining

Change to 2 strands of A held together and cont to use US size 10 (6mm) needle, knit each round until work in A measures 1" (2.5cm).

Mark end of last round.

Change to US size 13 (9mm) needle and knit every round until work measures 4⅞" (12.5cm) from last marker.

Mark end of last round.

Change to US size 10 (6mm) needle and knit every round until work measures 1" (2.5cm) from last marker.

Note: The lining is just a bit shorter than the base. *OK, now stop knitting.*

PATTERN NOTES

The puff base and lining are knitted together as a tube. The violets are then crocheted and lightly felted before they are attached to the puff.

*

Read through the entire pattern before you begin.

Leave your work on the needle, then leaving well over 36" (1m) of yarn for grafting the seam, cut off yarn. Don't seam it up now though, this will be done after the violets have been added.

TO MAKE THE TINY VIOLETS (MAKE 40)

Using US size I/9 (5.5mm) crochet hook and B, and leaving a 3" (7.5cm) yarn tail, ch 4 and join with a slip stitch in first ch to form a ring.

Round 1: Ch 1, 5 sc in ring, join with a slip stitch in first ch.

Cut off yarn, leaving a 3" (7.5cm) yarn tail, and fasten off. Pull the yarn tail down through the center of the violet.

TO MAKE THE LARGE VIOLETS
(MAKE 200 OR AS MANY AS YOUR YARN ALLOWS)

Using US size I/9 (5.5mm) crochet hook and B, and leaving a 3" (7.5cm) yarn tail, ch 4 and join with a slip stitch in first ch to form a ring.

Round 1: Ch 1, 5 sc in ring, join with a slip stitch in first ch.

Cut off yarn, leaving a 3" (7.5cm) yarn tail, and fasten off, then pull yarn tail through center.

Round 2: Using C and leaving a 3" (7.5cm) tail, join yarn with a slip stitch through center of ring, ch 4, [1 sc in center of ring, ch 3] 4 times, join with a slip stitch in first sc.

Cut off yarn, leaving a 3" (7.5cm) yarn tail, and fasten off. Pull both yarn tails down through the center of the violet.

TO ADD THE STAMEN TO THE VIOLETS

Make a stamen for each of the tiny and large violets.

Using US size G/6 (4mm) crochet hook and D, and leaving a 3" (7.5cm) yarn tail, ch 2 and join with a slip stitch in first ch to form a ring.

Cut off yarn, leaving a 3" (7.5cm) yarn tail, and fasten off.

Pull the yarn tails so the stamen pops into a knot, then tuck the stamen into the center of each violet using your fingers or the crochet hook.

We're making tails and we're gonna use em! The yarn tails will be used later to attach the violets to the puff base. They will also form the "stuffing" between the layers—*how handy!* You should now have six tails poking out the back of your large violets and four tails on the tiny violets. You may want to tie two of the purple tails together in a little knot to help secure the stamen, though felting should help with that.

TO MAKE THE LEAVES (MAKE 20)

Using US size 13 (9mm) circular needle and E, cast on 2 sts.

Work back and forth in rows on the circular needle as follows:

Row 1: K1, yo, k1. *3 sts.*

Row 2: Purl.

Row 3: Knit.

Row 4: Purl.

Row 5: K3tog.

Cut off yarn, leaving a long yarn tail, and fasten off.

Do not weave in the yarn tails.

HELPFUL TIP

If you are having trouble keeping the violet center nice and tight, as you work round 1 in B (the dark center), hold that yarn tail together with the ring as you work and work the single crochet stitches over the ring AND the tail held together. Once you have finished the round, pull the tail and the center will pop closed.

*

It takes some practice to get it right, but don't give up. Also, remember that felting will fix a multitude of oopsies!

I-CORD TIP

You can make an I-cord using regular needles, rather than dig out your circular needle or double-pointed needles. After you knit the 2 stitches, instead of sliding your work to the other end of your dpn or circular needle, just slip stitches purlwise back onto your original needle, bring the yarn around the back and start again. *YAY!*

TO MAKE THE VINES (MAKE 17)

Using US size 13 (9mm) circular needle and E, and leaving a 3" (7.5cm) tail, cast on 2 sts.
Work I-cord on the circular needle as follows:
Round 1: Knit, do not turn work.
Round 2: With the same side of the work still facing, slide sts to other end of circular needle, take yarn around back of sts, pull yarn tight and knit sts again, do not turn work.
Rounds 3 and 4: Rep round 2.
Round 5: With the same side of work still facing, slide sts to other end of circular needle, take yarn around back of sts, pull yarn tight and k2tog.
Cut off yarn, leaving a 3" (7.5cm) yarn tail, and fasten off.
Do not weave in the yarn tails.

TO FELT THE VIOLETS, LEAVES, AND VINES

Pop your first violet into the bowl of super hot water. Fish it out and wring most of the water out. You don't want the violet to be drenched—instead, damp is perfect. Place a dab of hand soap on your finger and tap-tap-tap it onto the center of the violet. Roll the violet between the palms of your hand for about 20 seconds. Now rinse.
The violet may have closed up into a bud, so just prise it back open and press the face flat to make a pretty shape. Separate out the yarn tails and then set the violet out on the towel to dry.
Felt all the violets, leaves, and vines in the same way. After felting, cut the tail at the tip of each leaf and shape the leaf into a little curl. They will then dry into shape.
Cute!

TO ATTACH THE VIOLETS, LEAVES, AND VINES TO THE PUFF BASE

Place a violet on the right side of the puff base, not the lining. Using a small crochet hook, pull half of the number of tails from the violet through to the wrong side. Do the same with the remaining tails from the violet, but approximately 1" (2.5cm) away from the first set of tails. Reach in and tie the two sets of tails in a double knot. Reserving approximately six large violets, four tiny violets, and four leaves that you will attach to the seamed edge later, tie on all the remaining violets and leaves in the same way, arranging them so that no area is left too sparse.

Finally, attach the vines as U-shaped loops by tying their tails to the nearby tails of violets.

The vines should look like tiny Loch Ness Monster humps, rising up out of the sea of violets here and there.

TO GRAFT THE PUFF SEAM

Fold back the lining and tuck it inside the puff base with wrong sides together. If you find you have a slightly lumpy looking puff, don't dismay. Rearrange the tails of the violets, leaves, and vines so they are evenly distributed and the puff looks smooth.

Remove the waste yarn from the open or provisional cast-on stitches of the puff base and place the live sts on a spare circular needle. Line up the needle points of the needle holding the cast-on stitches with the needle points already holding the lining stitches, with the wrong sides of the knitting together.

Thread the long tail from the lining stitches onto a blunt-ended yarn needle.

With the right side of the puff base facing you and the circular knitting needles in your left hand and the yarn needle in your right hand, graft the puff base and lining edges together using Kitchener stitch as follows:

Kitchener stitch set-up

1. Go into the first stitch on the needle closest to you as if to purl the stitch. Leave the stitch on the needle.
2. Go into the first stitch on the needle farthest from you as if to knit the stitch. Leave the stitch on needle. This sets up your seam.

Kitchener stitch

FRONT NEEDLE

1. Go into the first stitch knitwise. Slip the stitch off the needle.
2. Go into the next stitch purlwise. Leave the stitch on the needle.

BACK NEEDLE

3. Go into the first stitch purlwise. Slip the stitch off the needle.
4. Go into the next stitch knitwise. Leave the stitch on the needle.

Repeat these last 4 steps until all the stitches have been worked. Weave in the loose yarn end.

TO FINISH THE PUFF

Attach the reserved violets and leaves to the seamed edge. You will have to make the knots on the outside of the puff base and then push them and the tail ends through the puff base to the wrong side. You may want to pass a length of ribbon through the puff and hang it around your neck.

Now you are ready for some serious forest walking.

FAWN PONCHO

Shhh… A little fawn fell asleep on my poncho. Now it's a fawn-cho! Knitted top down, the fawn-cho then separates to create handy arm openings so you can carry your basket or kitty with ease.

OWL EXPERIENCE LEVEL

SIZES

	S/M	M/L
To fit bust	32–36"	38–42"
	81–91cm	96–106cm
Width measured	22"	24"
flat at base	56cm	61cm
Length from collar	20"	22"
	51cm	56cm

Note: Both sizes are knitted the same way until you see the ***. From that point on the directions for the larger size are given in parentheses ( ).

YOU WILL NEED

* **MC** 8 × 50g balls of an aran-weight wool yarn (4), such as Rowan *Tweed Aran* (105yd/96m per ball; 100% wool) in dusty green (780 Litton)—use two strands held together
* **CC1** 1 × 50g ball of a double-knitting-weight wool yarn (3), such as Rowan *Felted Tweed DK* (191yd/175m per ball; 50% merino, 25% alpaca, 25% viscose) in toffee (160 Gilt)—use three strands held together
* **CC2** 1 × 50g ball of a double-knitting-weight wool yarn (3), such as Rowan *Felted Tweed DK* (191yd/175m per ball; 50% merino, 25% alpaca, 25% viscose) in light brown (175 Cinnamon)—use three strands held together
* **CC3** Small amount of an aran-weight wool yarn (4), such as Rowan *Tweed Aran* (105yd/96m per ball; 100% wool) in off-white (770 Arncliffe), for ears, spots, chin, and tail—use two strands held together
* **CC4** Small amount of an aran-weight mohair-mix yarn (4), such as Rowan *Kid Classic* (153yd/140m per ball; 70% lambswool, 22% kid mohair, 8% nylon) in black (832 Peat), for nose and eyes—use two strands held together
* **CC5** Small amount of an aran-weight wool yarn (4), such as Rowan *Tweed Aran* (105yd/96m per ball; 100% wool) in dark brown (771 Keld), for hooves and a few extra spots—use two strands held together
* US size 10½ (6.5mm) circular knitting needle, 16" (40cm) long
* US size 10½ (6.5mm) circular knitting needle, 24" (60cm) or 29" (75cm) long
* Stitch markers in different colors and blunt-ended yarn needle

GAUGE

13 sts and 18 rows to 4" (10cm) square measured over St st using US size 10½ (6.5mm) needles and MC held double. *Use needle size needed to obtain correct gauge.*

Ready? Let's go!

TINY OWL STITCH DICTIONARY

See page 9 for general knitting abbreviations.

TO MAKE THE PONCHO

The poncho is made starting with the ribbed collar and worked downward toward the bottom edge of the poncho.

Note: Begin with the 16" (40cm) circular needle, then switch to longer circular needle when necessary.

Using US size 10½ (6.5mm) shorter circular needle and 2 strands of MC held together, cast on 72 sts. Place a stitch marker at beg of round and join in the round. (Slip marker when it is reached at beg of each round.)

Rib round 1: *K1, p1; rep from * to end of round.

Repeat last round 6 times more, working a total of 7 rib rounds for ribbed collar.

Round 1: *K9, m1; rep from * to end of round. *80 sts.*

Place shoulder markers

Using different colored markers, place markers as follows:

Round 2: K20, place marker, k40, place marker, knit to end of round.

Note: You should have three stitch markers at this point—one to mark the beg of the round and two to mark the shoulders.

PATTERN NOTES

For the contrasting color yarns, if you can't find the exact colors you want in a bulky-weight yarn, use three strands of a double-knitting-weight yarn held together or two strands of an aran-weight yarn held together.

*

Both the S/M and M/L size ponchos use four balls of MC, however the S/M size only uses a small amount of the fourth ball. If you want to save some cash, you could work the collar, bottom edge, and armhole openings in a contrasting color.

Working intarsia in the round is much easier if you carry the MC wool behind as you knit across the fawn, wrapping it every few stitches. For the center of the fawn, you may find it easier to join new CC yarns at the beginning of each chart row and break it at the end. As for any places that seem overly awkward, don't be afraid to just knit stitches in a comfortable color and then go over the top in duplicate stitch with the correct color after the poncho is finished. This is suggested for the hooves.

Hey, when I finished my fawn he looked totally mangled at first! Intense blocking and "fixing" holes and crumples with duplicate stitch or tacking is a crucial step for most of us! Don't give up, OK?

Cont in St st (knit every round), work as follows:

Round 3: *Knit to 1 st before next marker, inc 1, slip marker, inc 1; rep from * once more, knit to end of round. *84 sts.*

Round 4: Knit.

[Repeat rounds 3 and 4] 5 times more. *104 sts.*

Begin chart

Begin chart (see page 39) on next round as follows:

Round 15: Knit to 1 st before next marker, inc 1, slip marker, inc 1, k4, place new marker, knit 41 sts of *chart row 1*, place new marker, k5, inc 1, slip marker, inc 1, knit to end of round. *108 sts.* (New stitch markers denote beg and end of chart.)

Cont in St st, working chart between markers on every round, AND AT THE SAME TIME on every odd round/row, shape shoulders as follows:

Knit to 1 st before shoulder marker, inc 1, slip marker, inc 1, knit to chart marker, work from chart; rep from * to *, then knit to end of round.***

Cont to work chart and increases as now set and AT THE SAME TIME on the following chart rows, work as follows:

On chart row 19 (25), skip the shoulder increases on this round.

On chart row 21 (27), work the shoulder increases as normal.

On chart row 22 (28), from this point on, stop all increases. *144 (156) sts.*

Leave shoulder markers in place until further notice and cont in St st until chart has been completed.

Removing markers for chart on next round, knit 4 (10) rounds in MC.

Divide for arm openings and work back in rows

Divide for arm openings and work back of poncho back and forth in rows on circular needle as follows:

Row 1: Knit to first shoulder marker, slip marker, k5, turn.

Row 2: P5, slip marker, purl to next shoulder marker, slip marker, p5, turn.

From now on slip first st knitwise on knit rows, and slip first st purlwise on purl rows.

Leaving the front stitches on a stitch holder or a long strand of waste yarn, work 82 (88) back stitches in St st for 26 (28) rows more.

Now cut off yarn and put the back stitches on a stitch holder or a long strand of waste yarn.

Work the front in rows

Place live front stitches on a working needle and with RS facing, join MC and work these 62 (68) front stitches in St st for a total of 28 (30) rows, so ending with a purl row.

Join front and back in the round again

Note: Because the rounds used to start in the center back, you will have one more row on one side of the arm openings. Ignore this annoying glitch that happens with spiral knitting, it will not be noticeable once we get the edges on!

Next round: Removing the shoulder stitch markers as you work, slip live back stitches back onto a working needle, knit across front sts and when you get to final stitch, knit across armhole gap into the first stitch of back, knit across back stitches, knit across next arm-opening gap by knitting into the first of the front sts to complete round. *144 (156) sts.* Place marker to denote the new round beginning.

Next round (dec round): K7 (10), *k2tog, k7 (10); rep from * to last 2 sts, k2tog (k2). *128 (144) sts.*

Next round (rib round): *K1, p1: rep from * to end. Repeat last round 6 times more for a total of 7 rib rounds.

Bind off loosely in rib.

TO ADD THE ARM-OPENING FLAPS

Pick up stitches along the arm openings to knit the edging flaps as follows:

Outside top arm-opening flap

Using US size 10½ (6.5mm) shorter circular needle and 2 strands of MC held together and with RS facing, join yarn and pick up and knit 17 (19) sts along outside edge of one arm opening, then turn and work back and forth in rows as follows:

Row 1 (WS): *P1, k1; rep from * to last st, p1.

Row 2: *K1, p1; rep from * to last st, k1.

[Repeat rows 1 and 2] 5 times more.

Bind off in rib.

Work outside top flap on other arm opening in same way.

Inside bottom arm-opening flap

Using US size 10½ (6.5mm) shorter circular needle and CC1 and with RS facing, join yarn and pick up and knit 15 (17) sts along the inside edge of one arm opening, then and work back and forth in rows as follows:

Row 1 (WS): *P1, k1; rep from * to last st, p1.

Row 2: *K1, p1; rep from * to to last st, k1.

[Repeat rows 1 and 2] 5 times more.

Bind off in rib.

Work inside bottom flap on other arm opening in same way.

Now you have two flaps competing with each other. Tuck CC1 inside flap down under and let MC outside flap rest on top. Whipstitch along the short side edges of both flaps to secure them down. Turn poncho inside out to secure CC1 flaps.

Yay, fawn-tastic! Now let's head off to the forest together wearing our fawn-chos!

IMPORTANT NOTES ABOUT THE CHART

1. Start at bottom right corner and read chart row 1 from right to left.

2. Work chart using the stranded and intarsia methods—i.e., carry your yarn in some places, other times work blocks of color in sections. It will help to carry MC with you across the wrong side of the fawn twisting it around the working yarn every few stitches, that way you will not have to join new MC at the end of the chart each time. For the center of the fawn, join in new CC yarns at the beginning of each chart row and cut them at the end.

3. While working chart, work all stitches in the color of the square and ignore the symbols.

4. Cover stitches with symbols afterward in the suggested color, using duplicate stitch or embroidery where noted.

5. Work all embroidery in the same thickness as you knit the yarn with, i.e., if you hold the yarn tripled to knit with it, then hold the yarn tripled to embroider with it.

6. To make white (CC3) spots round, work a running stitch, and then another running stitch overlapping the first.

7. At the last minute I stuck on a little white tail.

CHART KEY

☐ MC
▨ CC1
▨ CC2
☐ CC3
▨ CC4

▲ work duplicate stitch off-white triangle in CC3, and charcoal triangle in CC5
— embroider lines in CC2 over eyes, and in CC4 and CC5 over nose
● embroider off-white dots in CC3

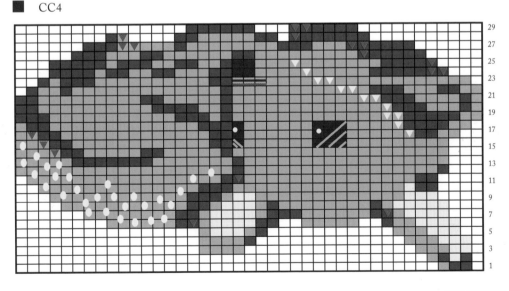

FREE RAPUNZEL!

Join the campaign to Free Rapunzel from her tower. Night and day she waits with naught but her spinning wheel to comfort her. Help us to free her. Wait a second. Up in a lovely tower with a spinning wheel and no distractions. Hmmm… On second thought, if we truly love her, maybe we should just leave her be.

OWL EXPERIENCE LEVEL

SIZE

One size to fit adult head 22" (56cm) in circumference

YOU WILL NEED

* 2 × 100g balls of a super-bulky-weight wool yarn (6), such as Rowan *Drift* (87yd/80m per ball; 100% merino wool) in brown (901 Driftwood)
* US size 13 (9mm) circular knitting needle, 16" (40cm) long
* Set of US size 13 (9mm) double-pointed knitting needles (dpns)
* Cable needle
* Ribbon for braids (optional)
* 6 stitch markers, 4 stitch holders (or safety pins), and blunt-ended yarn needle

GAUGE

12 sts to 4" (10cm) measured over St st using US size 13 (9mm) needles. *Use needle size needed to obtain correct gauge.*

TINY OWL STITCH DICTIONARY

T3F (twist 3 front)—slip next 2 sts onto a cable needle and hold at front of work, purl next st, knit 2 sts from cable needle.

T3B (twist 3 back)—slip next st onto a cable needle and hold at back of work, knit next 2 sts, purl st from cable needle.

C4B (cable 4 back)—slip next 2 sts purlwise onto a cable needle and hold at back of work, knit next 2 sts, knit 2 sts from cable needle.

C4F (cable 4 front)—slip next 2 sts purlwise onto a cable needle and hold at front of work, knit next 2 sts, knit 2 sts from cable needle.

See also page 9 for general knitting abbreviations.

Ready? Let's go!

PATTERN NOTES

First, the cabled brim (or headband) is knitted in one long strip. Then, the brim is seamed into a circle before stitches are picked up for the crown. The earflaps are picked up last and knitted down.

TO MAKE THE CABLED BRIM

The brim is knitted flat in a long strip.
Using circular needle, cast on 14 sts.
Work back and forth in rows on circular needle as follows:
Cable set-up row (WS): K3, p4, k2, p2, k1, p2.
Now work the next 8 cable pattern rows as follows:

Row 1 (RS): P3, T3F, T3B, T3F, p2.
Row 2: K2, p2, k2, p4, k2, p2.
Row 3: P4, C4B, p2, k2, p2.
Row 4: Rep row 2.
Row 5: P3, T3B, T3F, T3B, p2.
Row 6: K3, p4, k2, p2, k1, p2.
Row 7: P3, k2, p2, C4F, p3.
Row 8: Rep row 6.
Repeat rows 1–8 until strip measures 20" (51cm) from cast-on edge—it should wrap snugly around an average-size adult head.
Bind off. Seam the cast-on and bound-off edges of the cabled brim together using mattress stitch.

TO MAKE THE HAT CROWN

You are now ready to pick up stitches along the *top edge* of the brim for the hat crown. Which is the top edge? When looking at the brim, the wider, garter-stitch-looking border is the bottom edge, or hat opening, and the *shorter border is the top edge.*
Using circular needle and with RS facing, join yarn at back seam and pick up and knit 56 sts along *top edge* of brim for crown. Place a stitch marker at beg of round and join in the round. (Slip marker when it is reached at beg of each round.)
Knit every round until hat measures 5½" (14cm) from bottom edge of brim, then work as follows:
Round 1: Slip marker at beg of round, [k6, k2tog, place new marker] 6 times, k6, k2tog. *49 sts. Yep, that's seven markers in total, including the beginning-of-the-round marker.*
Round 2: Knit, slipping markers as you go.
Round 3: Slip marker at beg of round, [knit to 2 sts before next marker, k2tog] 6 times, knit to 2 sts before end of round, k2tog.
Switching to dpns when necessary, [repeat rounds 2 and 3] 4 times more. *14 sts.*
Round 12: Knit, removing markers as you go.
Round 13: [K2tog] 7 times.
Cut off yarn, leaving a long yarn tail. Using a blunt-ended yarn needle, thread yarn tail through 7 rem live sts, cinching them closed.

TO MAKE THE EARFLAP EXTRAVAGANZA

The earflaps are begun on the inside (WS) of the hat, 2 rows up from the garter-stitch brim edge, with the brim overlapping the ear flaps by ½" (2cm).

On the inside (WS) of the hat, measure 3" (7.5cm) from the brim seam along the bottom edge and 2 rows up, place a lock-stitch marker or safety pin there—this is where the first earflap will start. Measure a further 4" (10cm) from there and place another marker. This is where you'll pick up your earflap sts—between the two markers.

Using circular needle and with open edge of hat facing, join yarn and pick up and knit 14 sts between the markers.

Work back and forth in rows on circular needle as follows:

Row 1 (WS): [P2, k4] twice, p2.
Row 2: [K2, p4] twice, k2.
Rows 3 and 4: Rep rows 1 and 2.
Row 5: Rep row 1.
Row 6: K2, p2tog, p2, k2, p2, p2tog, k2.
Row 7: [P2, k3] twice, p2.
Row 8: K2, p2tog, p1, k2, p1, p2tog, k2.
Row 9: [P2, k2] twice, p2.
Row 10: [K2, p2tog] twice, k2.
Row 11: [P2, k1] twice, p2.
Row 12: K1, k2tog, k2, k2tog, k1.
Row 13: Purl.

Braid section

Knit the braid section loosely—if it is coming up too tight, try bigger needles.
Row 14 (RS): C4B, k2.
Row 15: Purl.
Row 16: K2, C4F.
Row 17: Purl.
Repeat rows 14–17 until braid section measures 14" (35.5cm).
Cut off yarn, leaving a 8" (20cm) yarn tail.
Using a blunt-ended yarn needle, thread yarn tail through live sts *starting with the stitch farthest away.* Cinch bottom of the braid closed and leave tail to hang down.
Work the other earflap and braid in the same way on the other side of the hat, the same distance from the brim seam.

TO MAKE THE BRAID TASSELS (OPTIONAL)

1. Cut 20 strands of yarn, each 12" (30cm) long—10 per braid tassel.
2. Using a blunt-ended yarn needle, thread each strand through the bottom of the braid and let it hang loosely so half of the strand is hanging in the front, and half in the back—the tassel will be 6" (15cm) long. It's not necessary to tie a knot; let the strands hang freely.
3. Cut a strand of yarn 22" (56cm) long for a "hairband." Wrap it around the top of the fringe a few times and tie a knot at the back. Thread the ends down into the tassel to blend in with the fringe.
4. Trim each tassel and tie a little messy ribbon around the top, just like Rapunzel would!

PS Oh, don't forget to add a poofy pompom to the top.

Thanks for joining the campaign to Free Rapunzel! If you are in a tower, hopefully this hat will help you pull up a prince. If you don't need no stinking prince, then I hope you will feel like a wild and free princess as you roam the moors with your long braids trailing behind you in the wind.

WOODLAND HOODLET

A cozy hoodlet made for picking berries in the woods and stopping to chat with deer along the way. Remember, deer love pretzels just as much as they like talking. Take plenty along with you when you go.

OWL EXPERIENCE LEVEL

SIZES

	S	M	L
Bottom of hoodlet measured flat	24" 61cm	25½" 65cm	27" 68.5cm

Note: Adjustments can be made when working the back piece to vary the size.

GAUGE

9 sts and 13 rows to 4" (10cm) square measured over St st using US size 15 (10mm) needles.
Use needle size needed to obtain correct gauge.

YOU WILL NEED

* 6 (7: 7) × 100g balls of a super-bulky-weight wool yarn (6), such as Rowan *Big Wool* (87yd/80m; 100% merino wool) in desired shade
* Pair of US size 15 (10mm) long knitting needles
* US size 15 (10mm) circular knitting needle, 24" (60cm) long
* Cable needle
* Stitch marker and blunt-ended yarn needle

PATTERN NOTES

The woodland cables are worked in short rows to make a nice curved yoke on the front of the cape, then the back is worked straight in stockinette stitch with a cable border along the lower edge. Don't be daunted by the rows of woodland cables. You'll find them easier than they look!

Ready? Let's go!

TINY OWL STITCH DICTIONARY

C4F (cable 4 front)—slip next 2 sts purlwise onto a cable needle and hold at front of work, knit next 2 sts, knit 2 sts from cable needle.

C6B (cable 6 back)—slip next 3 sts purlwise onto a cable needle and hold at back of work, knit next 3 sts, knit 3 sts from cable needle.

C12B (cable 12 back)—slip next 6 sts purlwise onto a cable needle and hold at back of work, knit next 6 sts, knit 6 sts from cable needle.

C12F (cable 12 front)—slip next 6 sts purlwise onto a cable needle and hold at front of work, knit next 6 sts, knit 6 sts from cable needle.

k1b (knit one back)—knit into back of stitch.

MB (make bobble)—knit into front, back, front, and back of next stitch (makes 4 stitches from 1 stitch), slip all 4 sts back onto left needle purlwise and knit 4 sts taking care to cross yarn at the back loosely, slip all 4 sts back onto left needle again, [k2tog] twice, then with tip of left needle pass second stitch on right needle over first stitch and off right needle.

p1b (purl one back)—purl into back of stitch.

w&t (wrap and turn)—move yarn to back of work between two needle tips, slip next stitch onto right needle purlwise, move yarn to front of work, slip stitch back onto left needle purlwise, turn work.

See also page 9 for general knitting abbreviations.

TO MAKE THE CAPE

The front and back of the cape are worked in one piece. The cabled front of the cape is worked first to fit from right to left across the front of the body, then the plain back with a cable lower border is worked to fit from left to right across the back of the body.

Front

Using US size 15 (10mm) needles, cast on 44 sts, using an open or provisional cast-on method. Starting with a purl row, work 3 rows in St st.

Cable set-up row 1 (RS): K6, [p1, k1b, p1, k12] twice, p1, k1b, p1, k4, p1.

Cable set-up row 2: K1, p4, [k1, p1b, k1, p12] twice, k1, p1b, k1, p6.

Note: The short-row sequence in the following woodland cable pattern is 4 rows each time. You will see that each wrap-and-turn (w&t) "row" is really 2 rows—this groups each pair of short rows together and condenses the pattern length.

Row 1: C6B, p1, MB, p1, C12F, w&t, p12, k1, p1b, k1, p6.

Row 2: K6, p1, k1b, p1, k12, p1, k1b, p1, C12B, w&t, [p12, k1, p1b, k1] twice, p6.

Row 3: K6, [p1, k1b, p1, k12] twice, p1, MB, p1, C4F, p1.

Row 4: K1, p4, [k1, p1b, k1, p12] twice, k1, p1b, k1, p6.

Row 5: C6B, p1, k1b, p1, k12, w&t, p12, k1, p1b, k1, p6.

Row 6: K6, [p1, k1b, p1, k12] twice, w&t, [p12, k1, p1b, k1] twice, p6.

Row 7: K6, p1, k1b, p1, C12F, p1, MB, p1, k12, p1, k1b, p1, k4, p1.

Row 8: Rep row 4.

Row 9: C6B, p1, k1b, p1, k12, w&t, p12, k1, p1b, k1, p6.

Row 10: K6, p1, k1b, p1, k12, p1, k1b, p1, C12B, w&t, [p12, k1, p1b, k1] twice, p6.

Row 11: K6, [p1, k1b, p1, k12] twice, p1, k1b, p1, C4F, p1.

Row 12: Rep row 4.

Row 13: C6B, p1, MB, p1, k12, w&t, p12, k1, p1b, k1, p6.

Row 14: K6, p1, k1b, p1, C12F, p1, k1b, p1, k12, w&t, [p12, k1, p1b, k1] twice, p6.

Row 15: K6, [p1, k1b, p1, k12] twice, p1, MB, p1, k4, p1.

Row 16: Rep row 4.

Rows 17 and 18: Rep rows 9 and 10.

Row 19: K6, p1, k1b, p1, k12, p1, MB, p1, k12, p1, k1b, p1, C4F, p1.

Row 20: Rep row 4.

Row 21: C6B, p1, k1b, p1, C12F, w&t, p12, k1, p1b, k1, p6.

Row 22: K6, [p1, k1b, p1, k12] twice, w&t, [p12, k1, p1b, k1] twice, p6.

Row 23: K6, [p1, k1b, p1, k12] twice, p1, k1b, p1, k4, p1.

Row 24: Rep row 4.

Row 25: C6B, p1, MB, p1, k12, w&t, p12, k1, p1b, k1, p6.

Row 26: K6, p1, k1b, p1, k12, p1, k1b, p1, C12B, w&t, [p12, k1, p1b, k1] twice, p6.

Row 27: K6, p1, k1b, p1, C12F, p1, k1b, p1, k12, p1, MB, p1, C4F, p1.

Row 28: Rep row 4.

Rows 29 and 30: Rep rows 5 and 6.

Row 31: K6, p1, k1b, p1, k12, p1, MB, p1, k12, p1, k1b, p1, k4, p1.

Row 32: Rep row 4.

Row 33: C6B, p1, k1b, p1, k12, w&t, p12, k1, p1b, k1, p6.

Row 34: K6, p1, k1b, p1, C12F, p1, k1b, p1, C12B, w&t, [p12, k1, p1b, k1] twice, p6.

Row 35: K6, [p1, k1b, p1, k12] twice, p1, k1b, p1, C4F, p1.

Row 36: Rep row 4.

Row 37: C6B, p1, MB, p1, k12, w&t, p12, k1, p1b, k1, p6.

Row 38: K6, [p1, k1b, p1, k12] twice, w&t, [p12, k1, p1b, k1] , twice, p6.

Row 39: K6, [p1, k1b, p1, k12] twice, p1, MB, p1, k4, p1.

Row 40: Rep row 4.

Row 41: C6B, p1, k1b, p1, C12F, w&t, p12, k1, p1b, k1, p6.

Row 42: K6, p1, k1b, p1, k12, p1, k1b, p1, C12B, w&t, [p12, k1, p1b, k1] twice, p6.

Row 43: K6, p1, k1b, p1, k12, p1, MB, p1, k12, p1, k1b, p1, C4F, p1.

Row 44: Rep row 4.

Rows 45 and 46: Rep rows 5 and 6.

Row 47: K6, p1, k1b, p1, C12F, p1, k1b, p1, k12, p1, k1b, p1, k4, p1.

Row 48: Rep row 4.

Rows 49 and 50: Rep rows 25 and 26.

Row 51: K6, [p1, k1b, p1, k12] twice, p1, MB, p1, C4F, p1.

Row 52: Rep row 4.

Row 53: C6B, p1, k1b, p1, k12, w&t, p12, k1, p1b, k1, p6.

Row 54: K6, p1, k1b, p1, C12F, p1, k1b, p1, k12, w&t, [p12, k1, p1b, k1] twice, p6.

Row 55: K6, p1, k1b, p1, k12, p1, MB, p1, k12, p1, k1b, p1, k4, p1.

Row 56: Rep row 4.

Rows 57 and 58: Rep rows 9 and 10.

Row 59: K6, [p1, k1b, p1, k12] twice, p1, k1b, p1, C4F, p1.

Row 60: Rep row 4.

Row 61: C6B, p1, MB, p1, C12F, w&t, p12, k1, p1b, k1, p6.

Row 62: K6, [p1, k1b, p1, k12] twice, w&t, [p12, k1, p1b, k1] twice, p6.

Row 63: K6, [p1, k1b, p1, k12] twice, p1, MB, p1, k4, p1.

Row 64: Rep row 4.

Sizes M and L only

Rows 65 and 66: Rep rows 9 and 10.

Row 67: K6, p1, k1b, p1, C12F, p1, MB, p1, k12, p1, k1b, p1, C4F, p1.

Row 68: Rep row 4.

Size L only

Rows 69 and 70: Rep rows 5 and 6.

Row 71: K6, [p1, k1b, p1, k12] twice, p1, k1b, p1, k4, p1.

Row 72: Rep row 4.

All sizes

Mark end of last row on all sizes—this marks beginning of back.

Back

Begin back patterns as follows:

Row 1 (RS): C6B, p1, knit to end of row.

Row 2: Purl to last 7 stitches, k1, p6.

Row 3: K6, p1, knit to end of row.

Rows 4 and 5: Rep rows 2 and 3.

Row 6: Rep row 2.

Repeat rows 1–6 of back pattern until back measures 19 (21: 23)"/48 (53.5: 58.5)cm from last marker (see Note below), ending with a RS row. Note: Piece should wrap lightly around your shoulders. Feel free to adjust accordingly here! If it feels like it may be too big, stop knitting earlier. Do not cut off yarn or bind off.

Have fun rambling through the forest with your new woodland hoodlet and don't forget to take the pretzels with you!

TO GRAFT THE CAPE SEAM

Before the hood can be added, the cape seam needs to be joined together. Undo the provisional cast-on and place the live sts on a long straight needle, with point facing toward cable border. Fold the cape in half with wrong sides facing each other. Align the needles, holding them in your left hand with the needle points pointing right so that the cast-on side is facing you—the working yarn will be coming off the first stitch of the cape back. Cut off the yarn, leaving a *very* long yarn tail for seaming. Thread the long yarn tail onto a blunt-ended yarn needle and graft the edges together using Kitchener stitch as follows:

Kitchener stitch set-up

1. Go into the first stitch on the needle closest to you as if to purl the stitch. Leave the stitch on the needle.
2. Go into the first stitch on the needle farthest from you as if to knit the stitch. Leave the stitch on the needle. This sets up your seam.

Kitchener stitch

FRONT NEEDLE

1. Go into the first stitch knitwise. Slip the stitch off the needle.
2. Go into the next stitch purlwise. Leave the stitch on the needle.

BACK NEEDLE

3. Go into the first stitch purlwise. Slip the stitch off the needle.
4. Go into next stitch knitwise. Leave the stitch on the needle.

Repeat these last 4 steps until all the stitches have been worked. Weave in the loose yarn end.

TO MAKE THE HOOD

Using US size 15 (10mm) circular needle, with RS facing and starting at center of front of cape, join yarn and pick up and knit 59 (61: 63) sts evenly along neck edge, ending back at center front. Place a stitch marker at beg of round and join in the round. (Slip marker when it is reached at beg of each round.)

Rounds 1–3: Knit.

Remove marker and *turn.*

Now start working back and forth on circular needle in rows as follows:

Next row (WS): Sl 1 purlwise, purl to end of row. Start cables as follows:

Note: From now on, slip first stitch knitwise on RS rows, and slip first stitch purlwise on WS rows (even when you are cabling). When you slip a purl stitch, make sure you pull it a little extra-tighter than normal.

Row 1 (RS): C6B, p1, knit to last 7, p1, C6B.

Row 2: P6, k1, purl to last 7 sts, k1, p6.

Row 3: K6, p1, knit to last 7 sts, p1, k6.

Rows 4 and 5: Rep rows 2 and 3.

Row 6: Rep row 2.

Repeat rows 1–6 until hood measures approximately 16" (40.5cm), ending with a row 2. (Ending on a row 2 is more important than having exactly the correct measurement—this way the cables will line up better when you seam the top.)

Cut off yarn.

Let your circular needle naturally fold in half with the wrong sides of the knitting together. Hold both needle tips together so the points are facing to right. You are now ready to work Kitchener stitch to graft the seam together at the top of the hood. Thread a blunt-ended yarn needle with a long length of yarn, and join the yarn to the edge of the knitting near the tip of the *back needle.* Work the Kitchener stitch seam as for the cape. Lastly, make a little tassel and attach to hood as shown.

MEOW MITTS

The sweet kittens on vintage Valentine's Day cards inspired these mitts. They're worked flat and sewn up leaving a thumbhole. They work out best if you sing the Meow Meow Meow Meow song as you knit them.

OWL EXPERIENCE LEVEL

Width	S	M	L	XL
SIZES	S	M	L	XL
Width	3"	3¼"	3½"	3¾"
	7.5cm	8cm	9cm	9.5cm
Length	4¾"	5"	5¼"	5½"
	12.5cm	13cm	13.5cm	14cm

Note: When deciding on which size to knit, place hand flat on top of a tape measure and measure width of hand at the knuckles. Mitts work best when they are quite snug.

YOU WILL NEED

1 × 25g ball of a 4-ply-weight wool yarn , such as Jamieson's of Shetland *Spindrift* (115yd/105m per ball; 100% wool), in each of the following eight colors:

* **MC** Dusty pink-beige (290 Oyster)
* **CC1** Light brown (107 Mogit)
* **CC2** Pale gray (105 Eesit)
* **CC3** Pinkish off-white (183 Sand)
* **CC4** Pale blue-green (769 Willow)
* **CC5** Dark blue-green (794 Eucalyptus)
* **CC6** Salmon pink (301 Salmon), for tongue
* **CC7** Brown-black (227 Earth), for eyes and nose
* Pair of US size 2 (2.75mm) knitting needles, 10" (25cm) long
* Two stitch markers and blunt-ended yarn needle

GAUGE

26 sts to 4" (10cm) measured over St st using US size 2 (2.75mm) needles and MC.
Use needle size needed to obtain correct gauge.

TINY OWL STITCH DICTIONARY

See page 9 for general knitting abbreviations.

TO MAKE THE LEFT MEOW MITT

Using MC, loosely cast on 40 (42: 44: 46) sts.
Rib row 1 (RS): *K1, p1; rep from * to end.
Rib row 2: *K1, p1; rep from * to end.
Starting with a knit row, work in St st for 6 (6: 8: 8) rows.
Begin chart
Set position for *chart for left mitt* and place stitch markers on next row as follows:
Row 1 (RS): K17 (18: 19: 20), place marker, knit 19 sts of chart row 1, place marker, k4 (5: 6: 7).
Cont in St st, working chart between markers on every row, until all 20 rows of chart have been completed, so ending with a WS row.
Cont with MC only and removing markers on next row, decrease as follows:
Next row (RS): Ssk, knit to last 2 sts, k2tog. *38 (40: 42: 44) sts.*
Cont in St st until piece measures 4½ (4¾: 5: 5¼)"/11.5 (12: 12.5: 13)cm from cast-on edge, ending with a RS row.
Next row (WS): *K1, p1; rep from * to end.
Bind off in k1, p1 rib.

TO MAKE THE RIGHT MEOW MITT

Work as for Left Meow Mitt, EXCEPT set position for *chart for right mitt* and place stitch markers on row 1 as follows:
Row 1 (RS): K4 (5: 6: 7), place marker, knit across 19 sts of chart row 1, place marker, k17 (18: 19: 20).

TO WORK THE SEAM

Use mattress stitch to sew the mitt seam. No matter what length you knitted, seam down from the top for ½" (1.5cm) and stop for thumbhole. Then seam up from bottom and stop to leave 2" (5cm) open for the thumbhole.

TO WORK THE EMBROIDERY

When working the duplicate stitches, hold the kittens upside down—so you are filling in the correct chart stitches.
Using CC7, duplicate stitch the eyes following the Embroidery Symbols Key. Pull the eye stitches quite tightly!!! If you do this, it will leave a big open spot of beige color in the middle, then after you put the mitts on, a pupil will appear. *Cool!*

Using CC7, embroider long straight stitches over the eyes as indicated to create a nice solid cat-eye look. For the nose, embroider long straight stitches in CC7 as shown on the chart. Lastly, duplicate stitch the tongue in CC6.

CHART NOTES

∗ Starting at bottom right corner on chart row 1, read all RS rows right to left and work in knit stitch; read all WS rows left to right and work in purl stitch.

∗ Use the stranded and the wrapped intarsia colorwork methods. Carry MC with you as you knit across the kitten, wrapping it around the working yarn every few stitches at the back of the work.

∗ Work each square in the color noted and ignore the symbols. Then work the symbols afterward following the Embroidery Symbols Key.

CHART KEY

☐ **MC**
■ **CC1**
■ **CC2**
■ **CC3**
■ **CC4**
■ **CC5**
■ **CC6** (knit in CC3, then cover with duplicate stitch in CC6 later)

EMBROIDERY SYMBOLS KEY

V work duplicate stitch in CC7 on eyes
< work long straight stitches in CC7 on eyes over the duplicate stitch
--- work long straight stitches in CC7 for nose

Hey, it's important to achieve the correct gauge otherwise your Meow Mitts might end up too tight or too loose.

CHART FOR RIGHT MITT

CHART FOR LEFT MITT

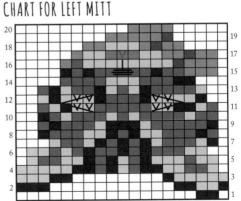

FAERIE WINGS

These light and simple faerie wings are a snap to make and a breeze to wear. You'll even forget you have them on, which is great when you are rambling through the forest—but it might get you some funny looks at the grocery store.

OWL EXPERIENCE LEVEL

SIZE

One size fits all, from children to adults

YOU WILL NEED

* 1 × 25g ball of a fine-weight mohair/silk yarn , such as Rowan *Kidsilk Haze* (229yd/210m per ball; 70% super kid mohair, 30% silk) in moss green (629 Fern), pale pink (580 Grace) or desired shade, for each pair of wings
* Set of US size 9 (5.5mm) double-pointed knitting needles (dpns)
* Set of US size 4 (3.5mm) double-pointed knitting needles (dpns)
* Approximately 2yd (1.9m) of 20-gauge strong beading/craft wire
* Wire cutters
* US size F/5 (3.75mm) crochet hook, for adding "veins"
* Stitch markers and blunt-ended yarn needle

GAUGE

11 sts to 4" (10cm) measured over St st using US size (9 5.5mm) needles. *Use needle size needed to obtain correct gauge.*

Note: This is a very loose web-like fabric so gauge is mutable.

Ready? Let's go!

TINY OWL STITCH DICTIONARY

CO1 (cast on 1 stitch)—this is an increase worked in the middle of a row as follows: loop working yarn around your left thumb (making a backward loop) and place new stitch on right needle. *1 new twisted st made.* (I chose this increase because it looks cellular.)

See also page 9 for general knitting abbreviations.

TO MAKE THE FAERIE WING (MAKE 2)

The wings are knitted separately in the round. Using US size 9 (5.5mm) dpns, loosely cast on 10 sts and divide them evenly on 3 dpns. Place a stitch marker at beg of round and join in the round. (Slip marker when it is reached at beg of each round.) Knit 4 rounds.

Round 5: *K2, CO1, k1, CO1, k2; rep from * once more. *14 sts.* Knit 4 rounds.

Round 10: *K3, CO1, k1, CO1, k3; rep from * once more. *18 sts.* Knit 4 rounds.

Round 15: *K4, CO1, k1, CO1, k4; rep from *. *22 sts.* Knit 7 rounds.

Round 23: *K5, CO1, k1, CO1, k5; rep from * once more. *26 sts.* Knit 7 rounds.

Round 31: *K6, CO1, k1, CO1, k6; rep from * once more. *30 sts.* Knit 5 rounds.

Round 37: *K7, CO1, k1, CO1, k7; rep from * once more. *34 sts.* Knit 4 rounds.

Round 42: *K8, CO1, k1, CO1, k8; rep from * once more. *38 sts.* Knit 3 rounds.

Now begin decreases as follows:

Round 46: *Ssk, k15, k2tog; rep from * once more. *34 sts.* Knit 1 round.

Round 48: *Ssk, k13, k2tog; rep from * once more. *30 sts.* Knit 1 round.

Round 50: *Ssk, k11, k2tog; rep from * once more. *26 sts.* Knit 1 round.

Round 52: *Ssk, k9, k2tog; rep from * once more. *22 sts.* Knit 1 round.

Round 54: *Ssk, k7, k2tog; rep from * once more. *18 sts.*

Round 55: *Ssk, k5, k2tog; rep from * once more. *14 sts.*

Round 56: *Ssk, k3, k2tog; rep from * once more. *10 sts.*

Cut off yarn, leaving a long yarn tail. Using a blunt-ended yarn needle, thread yarn tail through 10 remaining sts, cinching them closed.

TO MAKE THE WING FRAME (MAKE 2)

The wing frame measures 6" × 10" (15cm × 24.5cm) at widest points.

1. Using wire cutters, carefully cut 29" (73.5cm) of craft wire.

2. Begin to bend the wire in half gently—you are making the wing point. Make it as pointy or rounded as you like.

3. Secure the open ends closed by twisting the wire together to make a rounded end. The actual wing uses about 25" (63.5cm) of wire so you have 4" (10cm) of extra wire for secure wrapping.

4. Lastly, pull gently outward at the arrows. This gives the wing a nice bowed-out shape. Every wing is different!

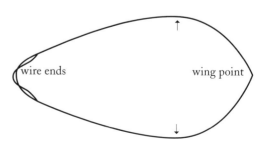

wire ends   wing point

PUTTING THE WINGS TOGETHER

1. Overlap wings at the round ends as shown.

2. Cut two 7" (18cm) pieces of wire and use them to secure the wings together in the two points where they intersect.

PATTERN NOTES

Forget about cutting up wire hangers and messing with difficult structure for the wing frames. I promise these are EASY!

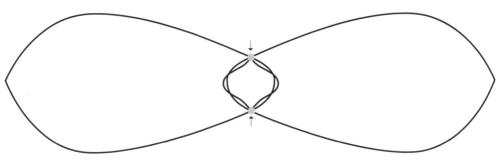

SLIPPING THE WINGS OVER THE WIRE FRAMES

1. Slip a knitted wing over each wire wing frame. (The increases go on the sides.) Don't be afraid to bend/pinch the wing frames closed gently to get the knitted wings over them. You can reshape them later. *Reshaping is key here!*

2. Using whipstitches, sew together the entire cast-on ends of the knitted wings. *Voila!*

TO SURFACE CROCHET THE VEINS

Using US size F/5 (3.75mm) crochet hook, work surface slip stitch for the veins as follows:
Hold the crochet hook in front of wings, and the yarn behind wings. Insert the hook through the wing, wrap the yarn around the hook, and pull a loop of yarn through. *Insert the hook again through the wing, a short distance away, wrap the yarn around the hook and pull a loop of yarn through the wing AND the loop on the hook. Repeat from * all along the veins, diving through the wing each time you pull up a new loop. You are basically crocheting a chain with the wings in the middle! *The veins are optional—the wings look cute with or without!*

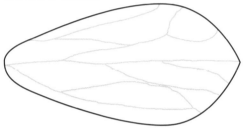

TO MAKE THE STRAP

Using US size 4 (3.5mm) dpns, cast on 4 sts onto one dpn.
Make an I-cord measuring 82" (208cm) long. The I-cord is a bit longer than needed on purpose. (See page 106 for how to make an I-cord.) Cut off yarn, leaving a long yarn tail. Using a blunt-ended yarn needle, thread yarn tail through 4 remaining sts, cinching them closed.

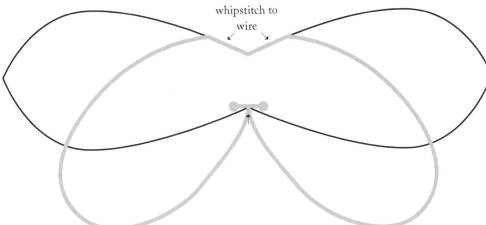

TO ATTACH THE ADJUSTABLE STRAP

Before you begin, make little overhand knots at each end of the I-cord.

1. Find the center point of the I-cord and whipstitch the center 4" (10cm) of the I-cord to the wire at the center top of the wings.

2. Let the I-cord make giant armhole loops and allow it to cross over itself at the bottom.

3. Make the straps adjustable by making a loose looped stitch over both straps (at arrow). The loop needs to keep straps in place but it should not secure them permanently. The overhand knots will stop the straps from slipping out of the stitch.

4. Try on the wings and pull the knots to adjust the strap size. The straps will be way too long, trim them shorter and re-knot. Bend the wings in a little bit so you have an easier time getting off the ground.

Happy faerie fluttering!

whipstitch to wire

DRAGON WATCHER'S HOOD

The Dragon Watcher's Hood will keep you warm while you wait for dragons to appear. It is fitted with three tiny bells in case the dragons you meet get feisty. Dragons love music so when you encounter one, just ring the tassel bells to relax them. Once the dragons are relaxed, they'll protect you forever and always toast your marshmallows to perfection.

OWL EXPERIENCE LEVEL

SIZE

26" (66cm) long from the brim fold to the point of the hood by 14" (35.5cm) high

YOU WILL NEED

* 3 × 100g balls of a super-bulky-weight wool yarn (6), such as Rowan *Drift* (87yd/80m per ball; 100% merino wool) in red (906 Fire)
* US size 15 (10mm) circular knitting needle, 24" (60cm) long
* Set of US size 15 (10mm) double-pointed knitting needles (dpns)
* Three small bells
* Stitch marker and blunt-ended yarn needle

GAUGE

10 sts and 13 rows to 4" (10cm) square measured over St st using US size 15 (10mm) needles.
Use needle size needed to obtain correct gauge.
Note: This fabric should be nice and dense. Don't be afraid to change needle size, if you must, to get correct gauge.

PATTERN NOTES

The hood is initially worked flat, starting at the brim, and then later joined in the round—so beginning with circular needles will make this easier as you'll eventually need to switch to using them. *Also, you'll be happy to know that the hat is 100% seam free! Yippee!*

Ready? Let's go!

TO MAKE THE HOOD

Using US size 15 (10mm) circular needle, cast on 78 sts.

Working back and forth in rows on circular needle, cont as follows:

Starting with a purl row, work 5 rows in St st, so ending with a purl row.

Folded brim channel

Pick up the bottom loop of each cast-on stitch, place it on the left needle, and knit it together with the corresponding stitch on the needle as follows:

Next row (RS): With RS facing, fold cast-on edge up behind sts on left needle (with wrong sides of knitting together), then using your fingers, loosen up loop of first cast-on st (behind first st on left needle) and slip this loop purlwise onto left needle, knit first 2 sts on left needle tog, repeat process for each st across entire row. *78 sts.*

This makes a curved brim with a channel running all the way around the brim of the hood. Later you will run your I-cord through this channel.

Beg shaping as follows:

Row 1 (WS): Purl.

Row 2: Ssk, knit to last 2 sts, k2tog.

[Repeat rows 1 and 2] twice more. *72 sts.*

Cont working in St st until work measures 9½" (24cm), ending with a RS row. DO NOT TURN at end of last row, but keep RS facing upward for next section.

Join hood in the round

Place a stitch marker at beginning of the round and join the work into the round by knitting into the very first stitch you knitted on the last row when working the first round as follows:

Round 1: Knit to 2 sts before marker, ssk, slip marker, k2tog.

Switching to dpns when necessary, repeat round 1 until 34 sts remain.

Round 20: Knit to end of round, slip marker.

Round 21: Knit to 2 sts before marker, ssk, slip marker, k2tog.

Repeat rounds 20 and 21 until 4 sts remain.

Last round: Ssk, k2tog. *2 sts.*

Cut off yarn, leaving a long yarn tail. Using a blunt-ended yarn needle, thread yarn tail through the 2 live sts, cinching them closed. Weave in any yarn ends. Sew a small bell to the hood point.

TO MAKE THE I-CORD

Using US size 15 (10mm) dpns, cast on 4 sts onto one dpn. Work the I-cord until it measures a 90" (229cm). (Make I-cord as explained on page 106.) Cut off yarn, leaving a long yarn tail. Thread yarn tail through the 4 live sts, cinching them closed.

TO FINISH THE HOOD

Using a large safety pin or threading device, slide the I-cord through the channel in the brim of the hood. For the tassels, cut six strands of yarn 48" (122cm) long (three for each end of the I-cord). Using a blunt-ended yarn needle, thread three strands, one at a time, through each I-cord end so they dangle equidistantly. Securing them isn't even necessary. Trim the tassels to the desired length and sew one small bell to each I-cord end with some spare yarn.

Remember, dragons love to dance, so don't be afraid to ring your bells!

MR. FOX STOLE MY HEART

(AND MINI FOX COLLAR, TOO)

Mr. Fox will steal your heart but don't worry, he loves you! He just wants to keep you warm and cheer you up all day. Note: No foxes were harmed during the making of this stole or collar.

OWL EXPERIENCE LEVEL

SIZES

Mr. Fox is stole-size and Mini Fox is a small collar. Note: Where instructions for stole and collar differ, collar instructions are given in parentheses ( ).

YOU WILL NEED

For Mr. Fox Stole

* **MC** 2 × 100g balls of a bulky-weight wool/mohair yarn (5), such as Rowan *Cocoon* (126yd/115m per ball; 80% merino wool, 20% kid mohair) in tan (815 Amber) or in beige (806 Frost)
* **CC1** 1 × 50g ball of an aran-weight alpaca/cotton yarn (4), such as Rowan *Alpaca Cotton*, (148yd/135m per ball; 72% alpaca, 28% cotton) in off-white (400 Rice), for chin and tip of tail—use two strands held together
* **CC2** 1 × 50g ball of an aran-weight wool/mohair yarn (4), such as Rowan *Kid Classic* (153yd/140m per ball; 70% wool, 22% kid mohair, 8% nylon) in charcoal (831 Smoke), for ears and feet—use two strands held together
* Pair of US size 10½ (7mm) knitting needles
* Set of US size 10½ (7mm) dpns

For Mini Fox Collar

A fingering-weight wool yarn (1), such as Jamieson's of Shetland *Spindrift* (115yd/105m per ball; 100% pure new wool) in each of the following colors:

* **MC** 2 × 25g in terracotta (1190 Burnt Umber)
* **CC1** 1 × 25g in pale gray (127 Pebble), for chin and tip of tail
* **CC2** 1 × 25g in brown-black (227 Earth), for ears and feet
* Pair of US size 4 (3.5mm) knitting needles
* Set of US size 4 (3.5mm) dpns

For both foxes

* 2 black buttons, for eyes
* Safety polyester toy stuffing, for fox head
* Magnetic fasteners (optional)
* Stitch markers and blunt-ended yarn needle

GAUGE

Stole: 14 sts and 16 rows to 4" (10cm) square measured over St st using US size 10½ (7mm) needles and MC.

Collar: 24 sts to 4" (10cm) measured over St st using US size 4 (3.5mm) needles and MC.

Use needle size needed to obtain correct gauge.

TINY OWL STITCH DICTIONARY

See page 9 for general knitting abbreviations.

Ready? Let's go!

TO MAKE THE BODY AND TAIL

The body is worked flat starting at the neck and the body and tail are worked as one piece.

Body

Using US size 10½/7mm (US size 4/3.5mm) needles and MC, cast on 16 sts.

Row 1 and all-odd numbered rows (WS): Purl.

Row 2: Inc 1, k to last 2 sts, inc 1, k1.

Row 4: Rep row 2.

Row 6: *Inc 1, k1; rep from * to end. *30 sts.*

Row 8: Knit.

For Mr. Fox Stole only

Row 9: Purl.

Row 10: * Inc 1, k1; rep from * to end. *45 sts.*

For both Mr. Fox Stole and Mini Fox Collar

Cont in St st until work measures 15"/38cm from cast-on edge, ending with a knit row.

Work decreasing section as follows:

Row 1 (WS) and all odd-numbered rows: Purl.

Row 2: *K5, k2tog; rep from * to last 3 (2) sts, k3 (2). *39 (26) sts.*

Row 4: *K4, k2tog; rep from * to last 3 (2) sts, k3 (2). *33 (22) sts.*

Mr. Fox should stay in place without a closure, but if you want to do some acrobatics, feel free to add snaps or magnets to his tail and chin to keep him secure. I used super-strong magnets on the Mini Fox Collar.

Row 6: *K3, k2tog; rep from * to last 3 (2) sts, k3 (2). *27 (18) sts.*

Row 8: *K2, k2tog; rep from * to last 3 (2) sts, k3 (2). *21 (14) sts.*

Row 10: *K1, k2tog; rep from * to last 3 (2) sts, k3 (2). *15 (10) sts.*

Row 12: *K2tog; rep from * to last 3 (0) sts, k3 (0). *9 (5) sts.*

Tail

Beg tail as follows:

Row 1 and all odd-numbered rows (WS): Purl.

Rows 2 and 4: Knit.

Row 6: K1, m1, k to last st, m1, k1. *11 sts (7 sts)*

Row 7: Purl.

[Repeat rows 6 and 7] 5 (4) times more. *21 sts (15 sts).* Mark end of last row.

Cont in St st until tail measures 2½"/6.5cm (2"/5cm) from marker, ending with purl row.

Change to CC1 (used double for Mr. Fox and single for Mini Fox).

Next row (RS): Knit.

Cont to work in St st for 5 rows more, so ending with a purl row.

Beg decreasing as follows:

Row 1 (RS): Ssk, knit to last 2 sts, k2tog.

Row 2: P2tog, purl to last 2 sts, p2tog.

Repeat rows 1 and 2 until 3 sts remain, so ending with a knit (purl) row.

Next row: S1, p2tog (k2tog), pass slipped st over. Cut off yarn and fasten off.

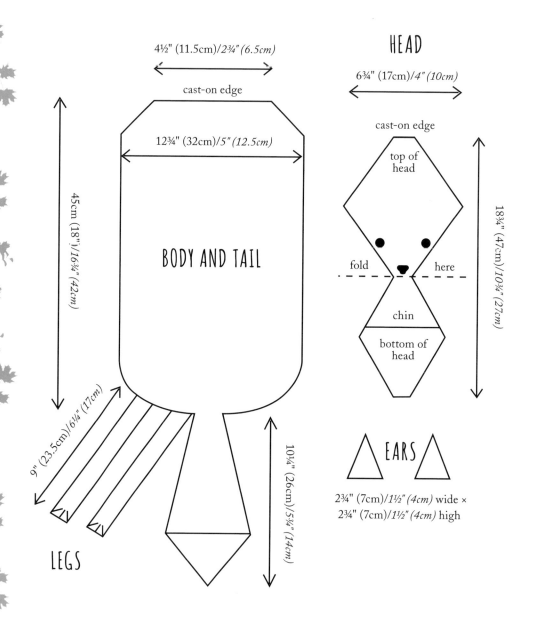

4½" (11.5cm)/2¾" (6.5cm)

HEAD

6¾" (17cm)/4" (10cm)

cast-on edge

12¾" (32cm)/5" (12.5cm)

cast-on edge

top of head

BODY AND TAIL

fold   here

45cm (18")/16¾" (42cm)

18¾" (47cm)/10¾" (27cm)

chin

bottom of head

9" (23.5cm)/6¼" (17cm)

EARS

10¼" (26cm)/5¾" (14cm)

2¾" (7cm)/1½" (4cm) wide ×
2¾" (7cm)/1½" (4cm) high

LEGS

Note: This diagram is for the Mr. Fox Stole and the Mini Fox Collar. The measurements for the stole come first and the collar measurements come second in italics.

TO MAKE THE HEAD

The head instructions are the same for both the stole and the collar, except for the needle size. The head is knitted in one long piece starting at the back neck, over the face to the tip of the chin, then under the jaw to the bottom of the head. Using US size 10½/7mm (US size 4/3.5mm) needles and MC, cast on 4 sts.

Row 1 and all odd-numbered rows (WS): Purl.
Row 2: Inc 1, place marker, k1, place marker, inc 1, k1. *6 sts.*
Row 4: K1, inc 1, slip marker, k1, slip marker, inc 1, k2. *8 sts.*
Row 5: Purl.
Row 6: Knit to 1 st before marker, inc 1, slip marker, k1, slip marker, inc 1, knit to end.
Repeat rows 5 and 6 until there are 24 sts, so ending with a knit row.

Face section
Removing the stitch markers on the next row, shape the face as follows:
Row 1 and all odd-numbered rows (WS): Purl.
Row 2: Knit.
Row 4: K9, k2tog, k2, ssk, k9. *22 sts.*
Row 6: K8, k2tog, k2, ssk, k8. *20 sts.*
Row 8: Ssk, k5, k2tog, k1, place marker, k1, ssk, k5, k2tog. *16 sts.*
Row 9: Purl.
Row 10: K to 2 sts before marker, k2tog, slip marker, ssk, k to end.
Repeat rows 9 and 10 until 4 sts rem, so ending with a knit row.

Chin
Removing the stitch marker on the next row, shape the chin as follows:
Row 1 (WS): Change to CC1 (used double for Mr. Fox and single for Mini Fox) and p4.
Row 2: Knit.
Row 3: Purl.
Row 4: K1, m1, k to last st, m1, k1.
Repeat rows 3 and 4 until there are 18 sts, so ending with a knit row.
Starting with a purl row, work 2 rows in St st.

Bottom of head
Change back to MC now and cont as follows:
Row 1 and all odd-numbered rows (WS): Purl.
Row 2: Knit.
Row 4: K1, ssk, k to last 3 sts, k2tog, k1.
Row 5: Purl.
Repeat rows 4 and 5 until 4 sts rem, ending with purl row.
Bind off.
Set head aside for now.

TO MAKE THE TOP HIND LEG

Using US size 10½/7mm (US size 4/3.5mm) needles and MC and with RS of body facing and tail pointing to left, count 10 (8) sts to the right from tail (along edge) and mark stitch, then starting at marked stitch, pick up and knit 10 (8) sts along edge toward tail.
**Starting with a purl row, work in St st for 2"/5cm, ending with a purl row.
Decrease row (RS): Ssk, knit to last 2 sts, k2tog.
Cont to work in St st until leg measures 5"/13cm (3½"/9cm), ending with a purl row.
Repeat decrease row once. *6 (4) sts.*
Purl 1 row.
Change to dpns of same size and CC2 (used double for Mr. Fox and single for Mini Fox) and work a 6-stitch (4-stitch) I-cord for 3½"/9cm (3"/7.5cm). (See page 106 for how to knit an I-cord.)
Cut off yarn, leaving a long yarn tail. Using a

HELPFUL TIP
If you don't have dpns, you can still work I-cord. After you knit the 6 (4) sts, slip them back onto the left needle purlwise one at a time. Then bring your yarn around the back of the stitches to knit them again.

blunt-ended yarn needle, thread yarn tail through 6 (4) live sts, cinching them closed.
Weave in yarn end.

TO MAKE THE BOTTOM HIND LEG

Using US size 10½/7mm (US size 4/3.5mm) needles and MC, count 8 (6) sts to the right of the first marker (along edge) and place a new marker, then starting at new marker, pick up and knit 10 (8) sts along edge toward top leg, picking up the last 2 sts under the top leg so they overlap a bit. Work as for top hind leg from **.

TO MAKE THE EARS (MAKE 2)

The ears are knitted separately in the round.
Using US size 10½/7mm (US size 4/3.5mm) dpns and CC2 (used double for Mr. Fox and single for Mini Fox), cast on 20 sts, leaving a 10" (25.5cm) yarn tail for sewing on ear.
Divide sts evenly between 3 needles. Place a stitch marker at beg of round and join in the round. (Slip marker when it is reached at beg of each round.)
Knit 3 rounds.
Round 4: K3, k2tog, ssk, k6, k2tog, ssk, k3. *16 sts.*
Round 5: Knit.
Round 6: K2, k2tog, ssk, k4, k2tog, ssk, k2. *12 sts.*
Round 7: Knit.
Round 8: K1, k2tog, ssk, k2, k2tog, ssk, k1. *8 sts.*
Round 9: Knit.
Round 10: [K2tog, ssk] twice. *4 sts.*
Round 11: [K2tog] twice, pass first st on right needle over second st and off right needle.
Cut off yarn and fasten off.

TO FINISH THE FOX

Fold the head in half at the nose. Using a blunt-ended yarn needle and MC, work the head seams at each side using mattress stitch, starting at the nose and working toward the back of the head. Leave a little space open at the back of the head and stuff the head lightly with toy stuffing.
Attaching ears
Keeping ears open at the bottom and making sure the ear decreases are facing front and back, whipstitch the ears securely to the head.
Attaching head
Letting the fox's neck naturally curl up a bit, angle the fox head as shown and place it on the body.
A nice angle will help Mr. Fox hug you better.
Sew the head to the body using simple whipstitches around the edges of the head.
Claws
Using scraps of CC1, embroider little claws on the two legs.
Nose
Using two strands of CC2, embroider a simple T-shape for the nose.
Eyes
Place the eyes between the eighth and ninth stitches back from nose and one stitch up from the jaw. Attach them with two strands of CC1 and a blunt-ended yarn needle. You can make the eyes indent and the fox face squish up really easily! Just run the yarn from the eyes straight out through the bottom/back of the head. Then pull the yarn gently until you get the right amount of "face squish." Secure the yarn under the head with a knot.

JUNIPER WISHING SCARF

Three long cables decorate this sweet soft scarf that uses a whole hank for fringe! Three is a magical wishing number so don't forget to wish on the cables. Though you'll have much better odds if you make your wishes on the fringe!

OWL EXPERIENCE LEVEL

SIZE

One size fits all (omit fringe for man's scarf) 6" (15cm) wide by 78" (198cm) long including fringe or 54" (137cm) long excluding fringe

YOU WILL NEED

* 3 × 100g hanks of a bulky-weight yarn (5), such as Misti Alpaca *Chunky* in (109yd/100m per hank; 100% baby alpaca) in green (7238 Chartreuse Melange)

Note: The scarf before the fringe takes 2 hanks, then you need one hank for the mega-fringe!

* Pair of US size 11 (8mm) knitting needles, 10" (25cm) long
* Cable needle
* Large crochet hook, for fringe
* Blunt-ended yarn needle

GAUGE

20 sts and 15 rows to 4" (10cm) square measured over cable pattern using US size 11 (8mm) needles. *Use needle size needed to obtain correct gauge.* Note: If you knit tightly, go up a needle size as this fabric should have loft.

TINY OWL STITCH DICTIONARY

C6F (cable 6 front)—slip next 3 sts purlwise onto a cable needle and hold at front of work, knit next 3 sts, knit 3 sts from cable needle.

See also page 9 for general knitting abbreviations.

Ready? Let's go!

TO MAKE THE SCARF

Using US size 11 (8mm) needles, cast on 30 sts.
Cable set-up row (WS): K4, [p6, k2] twice, p6, k4.
Beg cable pattern as follows:
Row 1 (RS): P4, [C6F, p2] twice, C6F, p4.
Row 2: K4, [p6, k2] twice, p6, k4.
Row 3: P4, [k6, p2] twice, k6, p4.
Rows 4 and 5: Rep rows 2 and 3.
Row 6: Rep row 2.
Repeat rows 1–6 until work measures 54" (137cm) from cast-on edge or until you've used up two entire hanks of yarn, ending with a row 2 or a row 4.
Bind off loosely in pattern.
Weave in any yarn ends.

TO ADD THE FRINGE

The fringe consists of 16 giant "fringe clumps," eight along each end.

1. Cut the entire hank of yarn into approximately 25" (63cm) lengths.
2. Gather up around 8–10 lengths of yarn per clump.
3. Fold the clump in half—this makes 16–20 strands per fringe clump. Attach each clump to edge of the scarf using a large crochet hook. To do this insert the hook from back to front through the edge of the scarf and pull the loops at the folded end of the clump through the scarf. Then pull the fringe ends through the folded loop and pull to tighten.
4. Attach eight fringe clumps evenly along each end of the scarf.

Happy fringe wishing!

CATCHING BUTTERFLIES

Catching butterflies is easy with these fingerless gloves. A delicate butterfly rests on the palm of each hand making it fun to flip your hands over to show off what you've caught! A tiny butterfly also decorates the other side.

OWL EXPERIENCE LEVEL

SIZE

One size to fit woman's average-size hands
3¼" (8cm) wide, measured flat, by 10¾in (27cm) long

YOU WILL NEED

* **MC** 1 × 50g of a fingering-weight wool yarn , such as Rowan *Pure Wool 4-Ply*, (174yd/160m per ball; 100% superwash wool) in desired shade
* **CC** Small amount of a fine-weight mohair/silk yarn (2), such as Rowan *Kidsilk Haze* (229yd/210m per 25g ball; 70% super kid mohair, 30% silk) in off-white (590 Pearl)
* Scraps of brown thread, or embroidery floss, for butterfly body
* Set of US size 2 (2.75mm) double-pointed knitting needles (dpns)
* Set of US size 3 (3.25mm) double-pointed knitting needles (dpns)
* Pair of US size 1 (2.25mm) straight knitting needles, for butterflies
* Cable needle
* Stitch markers, stitch holder, and blunt-ended yarn needle

GAUGE

28 sts and 36 rows to 4" (10cm) square measured over St st using US size 3 (3.25mm) needles and MC. *Use needle size needed to obtain correct gauge.*

Ready? Let's go!

TINY OWL STITCH DICTIONARY

C3R (cable 3 right)—slip next 2 sts purlwise onto a cable needle and hold at back of work, knit next st, knit 2 sts from cable needle.

C3L (cable 3 left)—slip next st purlwise onto a cable needle and hold at front of work, knit next 2 sts, knit st from cable needle.

See also page 9 for general knitting abbreviations.

See also page 9 for general knitting abbreviations.

With US size 2 (2.75mm) double-pointed needles and MC, loosely cast on 42 sts and divide evenly onto 3 needles. Place a stitch marker at beg of round and join in the round. (Slip marker when it is reached at beg of each round.)

Rib round: *K1, p1; rep from * to end of round.

Repeat rib round 10 times more—11 in total.

Change to US size 3 (3.25mm) double-pointed needles and knit 3 rounds.

Begin butterfly pattern

Round 1: K10, slip next 2 sts purlwise, *k12, slip next 2 sts purlwise; rep from * once more, k2.

Round 2: Rep round 1.

Round 3: *K8, C3R, C3L; rep from * twice more.

Rounds 4, 5, and 6: Knit.

Round 7: K3, slip next 2 sts purlwise, *k12, slip next 2 sts purlwise; rep from * once more, k9.

Round 8: Rep round 7.

Round 9: K1, C3R, C3L, *k8, C3R, C3L; rep from * once more, k7.

Rounds 10, 11, and 12: Knit.

These 12 rounds form the butterfly pattern and are repeated.

Repeat rounds 1–12 twice more.

Repeat rounds 1–9 once.

Shape thumb gusset

Cont in butterfly pattern as set, work as follows:

Round 10: Knit around and stop 1 stitch before end marker, inc 1 in last stitch, slip marker, inc 1 in next stitch (used to be first stitch of round 11).

Round 11: Knit around and stop 1 stitch before marker, place new marker (now referred to as right-hand marker or RHM), k1, remove old marker, k1, place new marker (now referred to as left-hand marker or LHM).

Round 12: Knit around to next marker (RHM), slip RHM, [inc 1 in next stitch] twice, slip LHM. Starting again with round 1 of butterfly pattern, cont as follows:

Round 1: Work in butterfly pattern to RHM, slip RHM, knit to LHM, slip LHM.

Round 2 (inc row): Work in butterfly pattern to RHM, slip RHM, inc 1, knit to stitch before LHM, inc 1, slip LHM.

Round 3: Work in butterfly pattern to RHM, slip RHM, knit to LHM, slip LHM.

PATTERN NOTES

These mittens are knitted in the round on dpns, but you could also use the magic loop method with a long circular needle. Keep a careful eye on your gauge. Even though this is fingering-weight wool yarn, it is NOT knitted to sock gauge (tight). Make sure to work a gauge swatch and move to a larger needle size if necessary, to obtain the correct gauge. Gloves should then be blocked to given measurements before the butterflies are attached.

Round 4 (inc row): Work in butterfly pattern to RHM, slip RHM, inc 1, knit to stitch before LHM, inc 1, slip LHM.

Cont working butterfly pattern as set at beginning of each round up to RHM, and AT THE SAME TIME knit thumb gusset stitches between RHM and LHM on odd rows and work thumb gusset increases between RHM and LHM on even rows as set until butterfly pattern round 8 has been completed. There are now *12 thumb gusset sts.*

Cont working butterfly pattern over sts as set, and AT THE SAME TIME stop thumb gusset increases from now on and knit thumb gusset sts on every round until round 12 of butterfly pattern has been completed.

Cont as now set, work butterfly pattern rounds 1–3.

Round 4: Work in butterfly pattern to RHM, slip RHM, knit 12 gusset sts then slip them onto a stitch holder and remove RHM, slip LHM (this marker now marks end/beg of round).

Complete top of mitten

Join back in the round. *42 sts.*

Work butterfly pattern rounds 5–12 on these 42 sts.

Change to US size 2 (2.75mm) double-pointed needles and work ribbing as follows:

Rib round: *K1, p1; rep from * to end of round.

Repeat rib round 3 times more.

Bind off loosely in rib.

Complete thumb

Using US size 2 (2.75mm) double-pointed needles, start at the thumb crease and slip 12 sts off of stitch holder and onto 3 dpns, join in MC and pick up and knit 2 sts from crease of thumb, then join in the round. *14 sts.*

Work ribbing as follows:

Rib round: *K1, p1; rep from * to end of round.

Repeat rib round 3 times more.

Bind off in rib.

Using US size 1 (2.25mm) needles and CC, cast on 12 sts.

Rows 1 and 2: Knit.

The two thumb gusset markers—right-hand marker (RHM) and left-hand marker (LHM)—will help you position the thumb gusset increases. You can use a different color for each marker to make it easy to remember which is which.

Row 3: K2tog, knit to last 2 sts, k2tog.
Row 4: Knit.
Rows 5 and 6: Rep rows 3 and 4. *8 sts.*
Row 7: Knit.
Row 8: Inc 1, knit to last 2 sts, inc 1, k1.
Rows 9 and 10: Rep rows 7 and 8. *12 sts.*
Knit 2 rows.
Bind off, leaving a long yarn tail for attaching butterfly to glove.
Cut a length of brown thread approximately 12" (30cm) long and wrap three or four times around the center of the butterfly to create the body. Tie the thread ends in a knot and hide ends.

Using US size 1 (2.25mm) needles and CC, cast on 8 sts.
Row 1: Knit.
Row 2: K2tog, knit to last 2 sts, k2tog. *6 sts.*
Rows 3, 4, and 5: Knit.
Row 6: Inc 1, knit to last 2 sts, inc 1, k1. *8 sts.*
Knit 1 row.
Bind off, leaving a long yarn tail for attaching butterfly to glove.
Create body as for the large butterfly.
ahem... I mean "catching"...
Block mitts to given measurements (see Size)

before adding butterflies.
Use a blunt-ended yarn needle and the yarn tails on the butterflies to sew them on. Stitch the large butterflies to the palm of each hand below the ribbing at the bound-off end and stitch the small butterflies to the back of each hand below the index finger. (Try them on first to get the placement right!)

*Wow, you didn't even need a net!
Have fun catching butterflies and remember
to set them free again before you go to sleep!*

GARDEN GATE & IVY

Everyone knows the luckiest vines get to climb all over garden gates. The inside of this reversible cowl is lined with garden gate pinstripes. The outside is rightly rambling with climbing filigree and ivy vines.

OWL EXPERIENCE LEVEL

SIZE

Approximately 11" (28cm) wide, measured flat, by 6" (15cm) high

YOU WILL NEED

1 × 100g hank of a worsted-weight yarn (4), such as Berroco *Ultra Alpaca* (215yd/198m per hank; 50% alpaca, 50% wool) in each of the following two colors:

* **MC** Tan (6208 Couscous)
* **CC1** Green (6275 Pea Soup Mix)
* US size 8 (5mm) circular knitting needle, 24" (60cm) long
* Spare circular knitting needle, similar in size, for grafting seam together
* Crochet hook, for working provisional cast-on chain (optional)
* Stitch markers and blunt-ended yarn needle

GAUGE

20 sts and 26 rows to 4" (10cm) square measured over St st using US size 8 (5mm) needles and MC.
Use needle size needed to obtain correct gauge.

TINY OWL STITCH DICTIONARY

See also page 9 for general knitting abbreviations.

PATTERN NOTES

This cowl is knitted in the round like a tall tube. It starts at the bottom of the filigree section and works through the chart, and then the pinstripe pattern begins. The cowl is then folded in upon itself and the live stitches are grafted together seamlessly with Kitchener stitch.

Ready? Let's go!

TO MAKE THE COWL

Using US size 8 (5mm) circular needle and MC, cast on 106 sts, using a provisional cast-on method. *(My preferred provisional cast-on method is to crochet a loose chain and pick up stitches into the back bumps of the chain.)* Place a stitch marker at beg of round and join in the round. (Slip marker when it is reached at beg of each round.)

Knit 2 rounds.

Position the filigree chart as follows:

Next round: *Using MC or CC as indicated, knit all 53 sts of chart row 1 from right to left*, place marker; rep from * to * once more.

Cont as set until all 29 chart rows have been completed. Cut off CC and cont with MC only.

Removing center marker on next round, knit 4 rounds.

Next round: *K24, k2tog, k25, k2tog; rep from * once more. *102 sts.*

Using MC and CC, beg pinstripe pattern as follows:

Round 1: *K2 with MC, k1 with CC; rep from * to end of round.

Repeat last round until pinstripes measure the exact same length as the filigree pattern from tip to tip of green—mine was about 5½" (14cm) so my pinstripes are 5½" (14cm) tall.

Cut off CC and cont with MC only.

Next round: K26, m1, k25, m1; rep from * once more. *106 sts.*

Cut off yarn, leaving a yarn tail that is at least 3½yd (3m) long for working the Kitchener stitch seam. *You'll need it!*

HELPFUL TIPS ON SEAMLESS JOGGING

Q. DEAR TINY OWL, EVERY TIME I START A NEW ROUND MY PATTERN LOOKS FUNNY BECAUSE IT'S JOGGING! HOW DO I MAKE IT STOP?

A. Because you are knitting in the round, you are knitting in a spiral and that makes the pattern stagger or jog. It's simple to fix! About every five rounds or so work a little magic trick as follows:

1. Stop after marker. *You are at the first stitch of the next round.*

2. Go down below that stitch and grab the right-hand side of the stich in the **row below**.

3. Place it on your left needle. *You now have a clump of 2 stitches.* Knit them together.

As a result, the first row of your pattern will be a little bit "shorter" than the rest of the rows in your cowl and that gives the illusion that the stitches line up. *Cool huh?*

TO GET READY TO WORK THE KITCHENER STITCH SEAM

1. Remove the provisional cast-on and place the live stitches on a spare circular needle. Be sure the needle points are in line with the working needles.

2. Fold the pinstripe section inside the filigree section (with the wrong sides of the knitting together), so your needles are cozily lined up next to each other.

3. Align your work so the filigree section is facing you and you're holding both needles in your left hand. The needle points are pointing to the right and the long yarn tail is coming off of the back needle (from the pinstripe section.)

4. Thread the yarn tail onto a blunt-ended yarn needle and work Kitchener stitch as given on page 31.

Q. OH, BEFORE I START, HOW LOOSE SHOULD MY KITCHENER STITCH ROW BE?

A. Good question, the Kitchener stitch row should look just like a row of knitted stitches. If you are nervous about it, keep it loose at first, you can always go back and toggle and tighten the row to the correct tension when you're finished.

CHART NOTES

Follow the chart starting at the bottom right corner each time and reading from right to left. The chart is worked entirely in knit stitch. The chart is worked *twice* during each round— over the 106 stitches. Work CC where noted and take care not to pull floats at the back of the work too tightly!

CHART KEY

☐ MC
■ CC

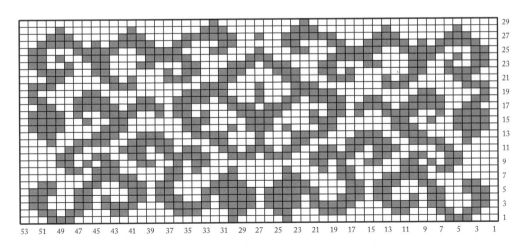

SEEDPOD PURSE

What do faeries carry in their seedpod purses? Why I don't think they would mind one bit if I told you. Buttons, feathers, jingle bells, cat whiskers, toadstools, pebbles, seeds, knots, dimes, and fishhooks. Oops, I shouldn't have said that.

OWL EXPERIENCE LEVEL

SIZE

8" (20cm) wide by 11" (28cm) tall, including tassel
Big enough to carry a medium sized hedgehog!

YOU WILL NEED

* 1 × 100g hank of a heavy-worsted-weight "felt-able" llama/wool yarn (4), such as Cascade *Pastaza* (132yd/120m per hank; 50% llama, 50% wool) in dark green (045)
* US size 10½ (6.5mm) circular knitting needle, 16" (40cm) long
* Set of US size 10½ (6.5mm) double-pointed knitting needles
* US size P (10mm) crochet hook, for making strap
* Stitch marker and blunt-ended yarn needle

GAUGE

12 sts to 4" (10cm) measured over St st using US size 10½ (6.5mm). *Use needle size needed to obtain correct gauge.*
Note: For this purse, we are using a larger needle size than is normally used for this yarn so that the purse felts better. *Bigger holes, better felting!*

PATTERN NOTES

This little purse starts at the top (opening) and is knitted in the round. Be sure to use a wool or other yarn that felts. Add a few felted leaves for luck and don't forget the tassel!

Ready? Let's go!

TO MAKE THE PURSE

Using size US size 10½ (6.5mm) circular needle, cast on 40 sts. Place a stitch marker at beg of round and join in the round. (Slip marker when it is reached at beg of each round.)

Note: Switch to double-pointed needles later when necessary.

Knit 7 rounds.

Round 8: *K1, inc 1; rep from * to end. *60 sts.*

Knit 3 rounds.

Round 12: *K2, inc 1; rep from * to end. *80 sts.*

Knit 5 rounds.

Round 18: *K9, inc 1; rep from * to end. *88 sts.*

Knit 9 rounds.

Round 28: *K9, k2tog; rep from * to end. *80 sts.*

Knit 9 rounds.

Round 38: *K6, k2tog; rep from * to end. *70 sts.*

Round 39: *K5, k2tog; rep from * to end of round. *60 sts.*

Round 40: *K4, k2tog; rep from * to end. *50 sts.*

Round 41: *K3, k2tog; rep from * to end. *40 sts.*

Round 42: *K2, k2tog; rep from * to end. *30 sts.*

Round 43: *K1, k2tog; rep from * to end. *20 sts.*

Add the little point at the bottom as follows:

Round 44: Knit.

Round 45: *K1, k2tog; rep from * to last 2 sts, k2tog. *13 sts.*

Round 46: Knit.

Round 47: *K1, k2tog; rep from * to last st, k1. *9 sts.*

Round 48: Knit.

Round 49: *K1, k2tog; rep from * to end of round. *6 sts.*

Round 50: Knit.

Round 51: [K2tog] 3 times. *3 sts.*

Cut off yarn leaving a long yarn tail. Using a

blunt-ended yarn needle, thread yarn tail through 3 live sts, cinching them closed.

TO MAKE THE FRINGE

The fringe goes all the way around the purse opening.

1. For the fringe, cut 40 strands of yarn, each 4–5" (10–15cm) long.
2. Attach a strand of fringe into each stitch around the purse opening at about round 2. First fold the fringe strand in half, then insert a crochet hook from front to back through the stitch and pull the folded fringe loop through the purse. Draw the fringe ends through the loop and tighten.

Stop now and felt the purse before adding the leaves, strap, or tassel.

TO FELT THE PURSE

Felt the purse, either by hand or machine.
To felt by hand, follow the instructions for felting the antlers for the Deer with Little Antlers Hat on page 14. To felt by machine, follow the instructions for felting the Birch Scarf on page 113. Your purse will stay in the shape it dries in, so you may want to fill it with polyester stuffing while it dries.

TO MAKE AND FELT THE STRAP

The finished length of the strap is 45" (114.5cm).
Using US size P (10mm) crochet hook, loosely crochet a chain about 48" (122cm) long. Felt and shape the strap, rolling it between your hands like a pencil and pulling it gently to lengthen and smooth it. It won't shrink much lengthwise, but it will solidify into a nice thin strap. Using spare yarn, sew the strap to either side of purse opening.

TO MAKE AND FELT THE LEAVES (MAKE 3)

Using US size 10½ (6.5mm) circular needle, cast on 3 sts, leaving a long yarn tail.
Work back and forth in rows on circular needle as follows:
Row 1 and all odd-numbered rows: Purl.
Row 2: [K1, yo] twice, k1. *5 sts.*
Row 4: Knit.
Row 6: K2tog, k1, k2tog. *3 sts.*
Row 8: Slip 1 knitwise, k2tog, pass slipped stitch over.
Cut off yarn, fasten off, and weave in this yarn end.
Felt the leaves gently and be sure to smooth them flat before they dry so they don't crumple.
Using the long yarn tail, attach them to the strap.
I attached three leaves in a little bundle for luck.

TO ADD THE TASSEL

The tassel is not felted.
Cut 20 strands of yarn, each approximately 10½" (26.5cm) long. Align the strands and tie them together tightly in the center, leaving the ends of the tying strands for attaching the finished tassel to the purse. Fold the strands together at the tied center and wrap a length of yarn around the top to secure, hiding the ends of the strand inside the tassel. Trim the ends so the finished tassel is 5" (12.5cm) long.
Attach the tassel to the little point at the bottom of the purse…and away you go!

Fill your seedpod purse with all sorts of friendly things, not fishhooks. Those are totally dangerous.

OH MY BEAR!

This is a good sweater to wear in the woods if you are worried about running into a bear. If you see one, you can simply point to your sweater and explain that you are a long-time bear supporter. They might just see reason and offer you some porridge! I suggest sitting in your own chair though.

OWL EXPERIENCE LEVEL

SIZE

One size, a department store woman's Large
Note: This jumper is very stretchy and about 23¼" (58cm) wide across the front and 20½" (52.5cm) long from the point of the V-neck to the bottom edge.

YOU WILL NEED

* **MC** 16 × 50g balls of an aran-weight wool yarn (4), such as Rowan *Tweed Aran* (105yd/96m per ball; 100% wool) in dark brown (771 Keld)—use two strands held together

An aran-weight wool/mohair yarn (used double) (4), such as Rowan *Kid Classic*, (153yd/140m per ball; 70% lambswool, 22% kid mohair, 8% nylon) in each of the following three colors:

* **CC1** 1 × 50g ball in off-white (828 Feather)
* **CC2** 1 × 50g ball in tan (877 Mellow)
* **CC3** 1 × 50g ball in gray-brown (866 Bitter Sweet)
* **CC4** Small amount of a bulky-weight wool yarn in light gray, for top of nose (optional)
* **CC5** Small amount of a bulky-weight wool yarn in black, for nose, eyes, and cheeks

* Pair of US size 10 (6mm) straight knitting needles
* US size 10½ (6.5mm) circular knitting needle, 24" (60cm) long
* Stitch markers, stitch holders, and blunt-ended yarn needle

GAUGE

11 sts to 4" (10cm) measured over St st using US size 10½ (6.5mm) needles and MC, CC1, CC2, or CC3 held double. *Use needle size needed to obtain correct gauge.*
Note: This gauge creates a slightly looser fabric than is usual for a yarn of this thickness.

Ready? Let's go!

PATTERN NOTES

All the aran-weight yarn is held double throughout. Work the chart using the stranded colorwork and intarsia methods. Carry MC when it is not in use across the wrong side of the work, twisting every few stitches around the working yarn, but mostly, keep your color "section" in blocks. Some small areas of color are best created using duplicate stitch after the sweater is finished as shown on the chart.

TINY OWL STITCH DICTIONARY

w&t (wrap and turn)—move yarn to back of work between two needle tips, slip next stitch onto right needle purlwise, move yarn to front of work, slip stitch back onto left needle purlwise, turn work.

See also page 9 for general knitting abbreviations.

TO MAKE THE FRONT

Using US size 10 (6mm) needles and MC, cast on 64 sts.

Rib row 1 (RS): *K1, p1; rep from * to end of row.

Repeat last row 7 times more—for a total of 8 rib rows.

Change to US size 10½ (6.5mm) circular needle and work back and forth in rows on circular needle as follows:

Starting with a knit row, work in St st until piece measures 9½" (24cm) from cast-on edge, ending with a purl row.

Start chart

Position chart on next 2 rows as follows:

Next row (RS): K16 in MC; place a stitch marker on right needle, then reading chart row 1 from right to left, knit 33 sts of chart, place a stitch marker on right needle; k15 in MC.

Next row (WS): P15 in MC; slip marker, then reading chart row 2 from left to right, purl 33 sts of chart, slip marker; p16 in MC.

Cont as set in St st, working sts between markers from chart, until piece measures 16" (40.5cm) from cast-on edge, ending with a purl row.

Shape armholes

Keeping chart correct as set, shape armholes as follows:

**Row 1 (RS): Bind off 3 sts, knit to end of row. *61 sts.*

Row 2: Bind off 3 sts, purl to end of row. *58 sts.*

Row 3: K1, ssk, k to last 3 sts, k2tog, k1. *56 sts.*

Row 4: Purl.

Row 5: K1, ssk, k to last 3 sts, k2tog, k1.

Row 6: Purl.

Row 7: Knit.

Row 8: Purl.

Rows 9, 10, 11, and 12: Rep rows 5–8. *52 sts.*

Row 13: K1, ssk, k to last 3 sts, k2tog, k1. *50 sts.***

Keeping chart correct and changing to MC only once you have worked all 44 chart rows, cont working in St st without shaping until armholes measure a total of 4½" (12cm), ending with a purl row.

You should be done with the chart now. RAWR!

Shape left side of neck

The neck is shaped with "short rows" by wrapping and turning.

Note: You will see that each wrap-and-turn (w&t) "row" is really 2 rows—this groups each pair of short rows together and condenses the pattern length.

Beg shaping left side of neck as follows:

Row 1: K22, w&t, p22.
Row 2: K21, w&t, p21.
Row 3: K20, w&t, p20.
Row 4: K19, w&t, p19.
Row 5: K18, w&t, p18.
Row 6: K17, w&t, p17.
Row 7: K16, w&t, p16.
Row 8: K15, w&t, p15.
Row 9: K14, w&t, p14.
Row 10: K13, w&t, p13.
Row 11: K12, w&t, p12.

Bind off 12 sts for left shoulder and cut off yarn.
38 sts still on needle.

Shape right side of neck

Using US size 10½ (6.5mm) circular needle and MC and with WS facing, rejoin yarn to remaining 38 sts and working back and forth in rows on circular needle, work reverse shaping for right side of neck as follows:

Row 1: P22, w&t, k22.
Row 2: P21, w&t, k21.
Row 3: P20, w&t, k20.
Row 4: P19, w&t, k19.
Row 5: P18, w&t, k18.
Row 6: P17, w&t, k17.
Row 7: P16, w&t, k16.
Row 8: P15, w&t, k15.
Row 9: P14, w&t, k14.
Row 10: P13, w&t, k13.
Row 11: P12, w&t, k12.

Bind off 12 sts for right shoulder and cut off yarn.
26 sts left on needle.

Slip remaining 26 center neck sts onto a stitch holder (or a strand of contrasting cotton yarn) and set aside.

TO MAKE THE BACK

Using US size 10 (6mm) needles and MC, cast on 64 sts.

Rib row 1 (RS): * K1, p1; rep from * to end of row.

Repeat last row 7 times more—for a total of 8 rib rows.

Change to US size 10½ (6.5mm) circular needle and work back and forth in rows on circular needle as follows:

Starting with a knit row, work in St st until piece measures 16" (40.5cm) from cast-on edge, ending with a purl row.

Shape armholes

Shape armholes as for front from ** to **.

Cont working in St st without shaping on these 50 sts until back is one row shorter than front to shoulder bind-off, ending with a purl row.

Next row (RS): Bind off 12 sts, knit until there are 26 sts on right needle, bind off 12 sts.

Cut off yarn. Slip remaining 26 center neck sts onto a stitch holder.

Now a little bit of seaming.

Lay front and back on a flat surface, wrong sides down and so that the shoulders are touching.

Seam front and back together at the shoulders. (Don't sew side seams yet but you can pin them together to make knitting the hood easier.)

Hey, sorry about the porridge guys, I was hungry.
Do you mind if I take a nap now? This bed looks just right!

TO MAKE THE HOOD

Using US size 10½ (6.5mm) circular needle and MC and with RS facing, start at the left shoulder seam (don't forget, "left" means left if you were wearing it) and pick up the "bar" left behind from the "short row" just before the first center front neck stitch on the stitch holder and knit it together with the first front neck stitch on the holder, then continue across the front neck stitches on the holder in this way picking up each short-row bar and knitting it together with the corresponding live neck st (where appropriate) until all 26 live front neck sts have been worked, pick up and knit 2 sts over the right shoulder seam, knit 26 sts from the back neck stitch holder, pick up and knit 2 sts over the left shoulder seam. *56 sts.*

Place a stitch marker at beg of round and join in the round.

Knit 2 rounds, slipping marker from left needle to right needle each time it is reached.

Remove marker, k13, turn—you are at front center. From here work back and forth in rows on circular needle as follows:

PICKING UP STITCHES FOR HOOD

Each "bar" left along the edge of the front neck by the short rows looks like a little bump at the base of each stitch.
Pick it up with your right hand needle and knit it together with the next stitch on left needle. This makes a smooth fabric. If this step is confusing, just skip the bar stuff, it'll still be cute!

Next row (WS): Sl 1 purlwise, p55, turn.
Next row (RS): Sl 1 knitwise, k13, [m1, k4] 7 times, m1, k14. *64 sts.*

Slipping first stitch purlwise on WS rows and knitwise on RS rows, cont to work in St st on these 64 hood sts until hood measures 10" (25.5cm), ending with a purl row.

Shape hood

Beg shaping hood as follows:

Row 1 (RS): Sl 1 knitwise, k29, ssk, place marker, k2tog, k30. *62 sts.*
Row 2: Sl 1 purlwise, purl to end of row (slipping marker when reached).
Row 3: Sl 1 knitwise, k28, ssk, slip marker, k2tog, k29. *60 sts.*
Row 4: Sl 1 purlwise, purl to end of row (slipping marker when reached).

Cont as set, decreasing one stitch before and one stitch after marker on every RS row until 48 sts remain, so ending with a knit row.

Do NOT cut off yarn or bind off.

TO GRAFT THE HOOD SEAM

Prepare the hood stitches for grafting the hood seam as follows:

Slip 24 sts on either side of marker onto straight needles—with both needle points facing away from the center of the hood stitches.

Align the needles, with the wrong sides of the knitting together, and hold both needles in your left hand, points facing right—the working yarn will be coming off the back needle.

Cut off yarn, leaving a *very* long yarn tail for seaming. Thread the long yarn tail onto a blunt-ended yarn needle and graft the edges together using Kitchener stitch as explained on page 31.

CHART KEY

■ MC
□ CC1
▨ CC2
▨ CC3
▨ knit in CC1, then duplicate stitch with CC4
■ CC5
◉ knit in MC, then duplicate stitch with CC2
● knit in MC, then duplicate stitch with CC3
◘ knit in CC5, then duplicate stitch with CC1

TO MAKE THE SLEEVES (MAKE 2)

Using US size 10 (6mm) needles, cast on 28 sts.
Rib row 1: *K1, p1; rep from * to end of row.
Repeat last row 7 times more.
Change to US size 10½ (6.5mm) circular needle and work back and forth in rows on circular needle as follows:
Next row (RS): [K11, inc 1] twice, k4. *30 sts.*
Starting with a purl row, cont in St st until sleeve measures 8" (20.5cm) from cast-on edge, ending with a purl row.
Next row (inc row): K 1, inc 1, knit to last 2 sts, inc 1, k1.
Cont in St st and AT THE SAME TIME repeat the inc row on a RS row when sleeve measures the following lengths from the cast-on edge—10" (25.5cm), 12" (30.5cm), 14" (35.5cm), 15" (38cm), and 16" (40.5cm). *42 sts.*
Cont in St st without shaping until sleeve measures 17" (43cm) from cast-on edge, ending with a purl row.
Shape top of sleeve
Row 1: Bind off 3 sts, knit to end of row. *39 sts.*
Row 2: Bind off 3 sts, purl to end of row. *36 sts.*
Row 3: K1, ssk, knit to last 3 sts, k2tog, k1. *34 sts.*
Row 4: Purl.
Row 5: K1, ssk, knit to last 3 sts, k2tog, k1. *32 sts.*
Row 6: Purl.
Row 7: Knit.
Row 8: Purl.
Rows 9, 10, 11, and 12: Rep rows 5–8. *30 sts.*
Row 13: K1, ssk, knit to last 3 sts, k2tog, k1.

> ## HELPFUL TIP
>
> If you want your sleeves to be longer than 17" (43cm) from the armpit, feel free to add another ¾–1½" (2–4cm) of stockinette stitch rows, worked even, right before you begin shaping the top of the sleeve.

Row 14: Purl.
Repeat rows 13 and 14 until 16 stitches remain, ending with a purl row.
Bind off.

TO MAKE THE EARS (MAKE 2)

The cast-on edge of the ear is the top of the ear.
Using US size 10 (6mm) needles and MC, cast on 11 sts.
Starting with a purl row, work in St st for 4 rows.
Row 5: [P2tog] 5 times, p1. *6 sts.*
Row 6: K2tog, knit to end of row. *5 sts.*
Row 7: [P2tog] twice, p1. *3 sts.*
Row 8: Sl 1 knitwise, k2tog, pass slipped st over 2nd st on right needle and off right needle.
Cut off yarn and fasten off. Whipstitch the ears to the hood with the purl side facing front.

TO FINISH THE SWEATER

Construction time: Your shoulders are already seamed and your hood is on!
Lay sweater and sleeves open and flat and set in the sleeves, using your preferred sewing method. Sew from armpit to armpit all along the top of each sleeve. Once the sleeves are in, fold the sweater in half so it looks normal again. Now just sew up the side seams from the lower edge of the sweater to the armpit, then from the wrist to the armpit. *That way any fudging can happen underneath your arms. Cheeky!*
PS I used mattress stitch.

WANDERWILLOWS

Willow my wander wood wandering fair, with little white flowers
tucked in her hair. She withers, she wanders, she weaves, and
she roams. When the moon rises she makes her way home.
Or she'll go to a party.

OWL EXPERIENCE LEVEL

SIZE

To fit woman's average size
6½" (16.5cm) wide, measured flat, by 16"
(40cm) long
Note: The legwarmers can be knitted longer
if desired.

YOU WILL NEED

* **MC** 3 × 50g hanks of a worsted-weight
  alpaca-mix yarn (4), such as Berroco *Flicker*
  (189yd/173m per hank; 87% baby alpaca,
  8% acrylic, 5% other fibers) in brown
  (3317 Benno)—used double throughout

* **CC1** 2 × 100g hanks of a super-bulky-
  weight fur-effect yarn (6), such as Erika
  Knight *Fur Wool* (44yd/40m per hank;
  97% wool, 3% nylon) in beige (002 Flax),
  for top and bottom edging
* US size 10½ (6.5mm) circular needle,
  16" (40cm) long
* Cable needle
* Stitch markers and blunt-eyed yarn needle

GAUGE

14 sts and 20 rows to 4" (10cm) square measured
over St st using US size 10½ (6.5mm) needles and
MC held double. *Use needle size needed to obtain
correct gauge.*

Ready? Let's go!

TINY OWL STITCH DICTIONARY

C8F (cable 8 front)—slip next 4 sts purlwise onto a cable needle and hold at front of work, knit next 4 sts, knit 4 sts from cable needle.

MB (make bobble)—knit into the front, back, front, and back of next stitch (makes 4 stitches from 1 stitch), then with tip of left needle slip 2nd, 3rd, and 4th stitches on right needle one at a time over first stitch and off right needle.

See also page 9 for general knitting abbreviations.

TO MAKE THE WANDERWILLOWS (MAKE 2)

Using US size 10½ (6.5mm) circular needle and two strands of MC held together throughout, cast on 46 sts. Place a stitch marker at beg of round and join in the round. (Slip marker when it is reached at beg of each round.)

Knit 7 rounds, then remove marker.

K 17 sts, place a marker on right needle and stop. *(This is the new beginning of the round.)*

Beg cable and bobble pattern as follows:

Round 1: MB, k1, C8F, k1, MB, knit to end of round.

Rounds 2–8: Knit.

Repeat rounds 1–8 until leggie measures 12" (30cm) from cast-on edge.

Next round: *K1, p1; rep from * to end of round.

Bind off loosely in rib.

TO ADD THE CUFFS

Using US size 10½ (6.5mm) circular needle and CC, pick up and knit 25 sts evenly around the top (the bound-off edge) of leggie. Place a stitch marker at beg of round and join in the round. (Slip marker when it is reached at beg of each round.) Purl every round until cuff measures 4" (10cm). Bind off loosely purlwise.

Optional: If you like, work another smaller cuff, 1" (2.5cm) wide, in the same way around the bottom (cast-on edge) of the leggies.

Now you are ready to wander to a party! I mean to the library.

WILDFLOWER CROWN

With thin jewelry wire inside, the wildflower crown sits lightly but securely on your head. When you're gathering wildflowers in the meadow, you will forget you even have it on!

OWL EXPERIENCE LEVEL

SIZE

Adjustable to fit any head size

YOU WILL NEED

* **MC** 1 × 25g ball of a fingering-weight wool (), such as Jamieson's of Shetland *Spindrift* (115yd/105m per ball; 100% pure new wool) in desired shade
* **CC** 1 × 25g ball of a fine-weight mohair/silk yarn (2), such as Rowan *Kidsilk Haze* (229yd/210m per ball; 70% super kid mohair, 30% silk) in desired shade
* Two US size 2 (2.75mm) double-pointed knitting needles

* US size F/5 (3.75mm) crochet hook
* Approximately 26" (66cm) of craft or silver jewelry wire, 0.6mm in diameter
* Wire cutters
* Blunt-ended yarn needle

GAUGE

28 sts to 4" (10cm) measured over St st using US size 2 (2.75mm) needles and MC. *Use needle size needed to obtain correct gauge.*

TINY OWL STITCH DICTIONARY

See page 9 for general knitting abbreviations.

Ready? Let's go!

PATTERN NOTES

This is a knitted I-cord with crocheted
flowers attached. Fine-gauge jewelry wire
is inserted for some structure.

*

For extra fun, make two or three crowns
and twist them together!

TO MAKE THE CROWN

Using US size 2 (2.75mm) double-pointed needles
and MC, cast on 4 sts.

Work an I-cord until the cord sits gently around
your head without stretching it—for example,
for an average-size adult head, a cord 22"
(56cm) long, or for a child 3–10 years old, a cord
approximately 19½" (49.5cm) long.

Cut off yarn, leaving a long yarn tail.

Using a blunt-ended yarn needle, thread yarn tail
through live sts, gently cinching them closed.

NEED HELP WITH AN I-CORD?

1. Using double-pointed needles, cast
4 stitches onto one dpn.

2. Knit 4 stitches as normal, but do not turn
the work at the end of the row.

3. *With the same side of the work still
facing you, slide the stitches to the other
end of the dpn.

4. The stitches are ready to knit again, but
now the yarn is at the wrong end. That's
OK! Gently bring the yarn behind the
work and knit the same 4 stitches again.

5. Repeat from * until your cord is the
length you want. Then either bind off
OR cut off the yarn and thread the yarn
tail through the live stitches, cinching
them closed.

TO FINISH THE CROWN

1. Cut a piece of jewelry wire to measure 3"
(7.5cm) longer than your I-cord. Bend one
end of the wire into a little loop. Slide the
looped end of the wire down through
the center of the I-cord.

2. Wrap the crown around your head to
determine how big it should be. The crown
should rest gently on your head and not be
too tight.

3. Secure the wire by twisting it securely
upon itself. Trim any sharp edges with wire
cutters and curl the ends in for safety.

4. Now whipstitch the ends of the I-cord
together to form a ring. Weave in
any yarn ends.

TO ADD THE WILDFLOWERS

The wildflowers are crocheted directly *onto* the crown.

Using US size F/5 (3.75mm) crochet hook and CC, join yarn with a slip stitch in any knit stitch on the outside edge of the crown. (You will work the first three petals into this same crown knit stitch and the next four petals into a neighboring crown knit stitch.)

Making the flower: *[Ch 5, 1 slip stitch in same crown knit stitch] 3 times, turn crown so petals are facing downward and work 1 slip stitch in crown knit stitch on outside edge of crown just above where last slip stitch was worked, [5 ch, 1 slip stitch in same crown knit stitch as last slip stitch] 4 times. *7 petals made.* Fasten off.

Seven is a faery number, so make seven wildflowers evenly spaced around the outside edge of the crown.

Notice: Wearing your wildflower crown will definitely attract faeries! Don't forget to offer them a nice cool drink.

SPIRIT OF THE BIRCH

The birch tree is a magical tree that symbolizes birth and new beginnings. My grandmother used to tell me to write my wishes on the little strips of bark that had naturally fallen off of the birch trees in her garden.

OWL EXPERIENCE LEVEL

SIZES

Finished felted scarf measures 3½" by 78" (9cm by 196cm), excluding fringe (longest tip of fringe is 11"/28cm)

Finished felted cuff measures 3½" by 4" (9cm by 10cm) or felted to fit

YOU WILL NEED

A bulky-weight 100% wool yarn (be sure it felts, see Pattern Notes) 5, such as Cascade *Ecological Wool* (478yd/437m per hank; 100% natural Peruvian wool) in each of the following two colors:

* **MC** 1 × 250g hank in off-white (8010 Ecru)
* **CC1** 1 × 250g hank in brown (8087 Chocolate)

Note: As you only need about one third of the 250g hank of CC1, you could alternatively find a smaller ball of a bulky-weight yarn or use some worsted-weight yarn doubled.

* **CC2** Approximately 20yd (20m) of a medium-weight synthetic eyelash (or fur) yarn (4), for edges and fringe
* US size 11 (8mm) circular knitting needle, 16" (40cm) long, OR set of US size 11 (8mm) double-pointed knitting needles
* Crochet hook, for attaching fringe
* Stitch marker and blunt-ended yarn needle

GAUGE

12 sts and 14 rows to 4" (10cm) square measured over St st worked in the round using US size 11 (8mm) circular needle and MC.
Use needle size needed to obtain correct gauge.
Note: This fabric should look loose, so it is better for felting. Don't hesitate to go up a needle size if you usually knit tightly.

Ready? Let's go!

PATTERN NOTES

This scarf is knitted in the round like a tube and then felted in the washing machine. The wispy spirit fringe is added afterward and slightly felted by hand. Be sure to check your white wool to make sure it felts. And begin by knitting the fun little Birch Cuff both to check your gauge and to make sure you don't run out of yarn when making the scarf.

TINY OWL STITCH DICTIONARY

fold stitch   go to the back of the work with your right needle and pick up a stitch from about 4 rows below the next stitch on the left needle, place it on your left needle and knit it together with the next stitch.

Note: The fold stitch doesn't have to be perfect. Feel free to stray from the charts as much as you want, as each birch tree is different. *Go with the flow and hear the spirit of the birch speak to you!* See also page 9 for general knitting abbreviations.

TO MAKE THE BIRCH CUFF

Set aside enough yarn to make the fringe for both the cuff and scarf.

Using 8mm (US size 11) circular needle (or dpns) and a strand of MC held together with a strand of CC2, cast on 25 sts very loosely. Place a stitch marker at beg of round and join in the round. (Slip marker when it is reached at beg of each round.)

Note: If you have trouble getting 25 sts around a circular needle at first, feel free to start out on double-pointed needles (or larger needles) if necessary and be loose. *It can be done. I did it!*

Round 1: Knit.

Round 2: [K8, m1] 3 times, k1. *28 sts.***

Cut off strand of CC2 and cont with MC only. Using MC, and introducing CC1 only where required, work from chart, starting with chart round 1 and ending with chart round 22. (See the Chart and Colorwork Notes on page 112.)

Bind off loosely in MC.

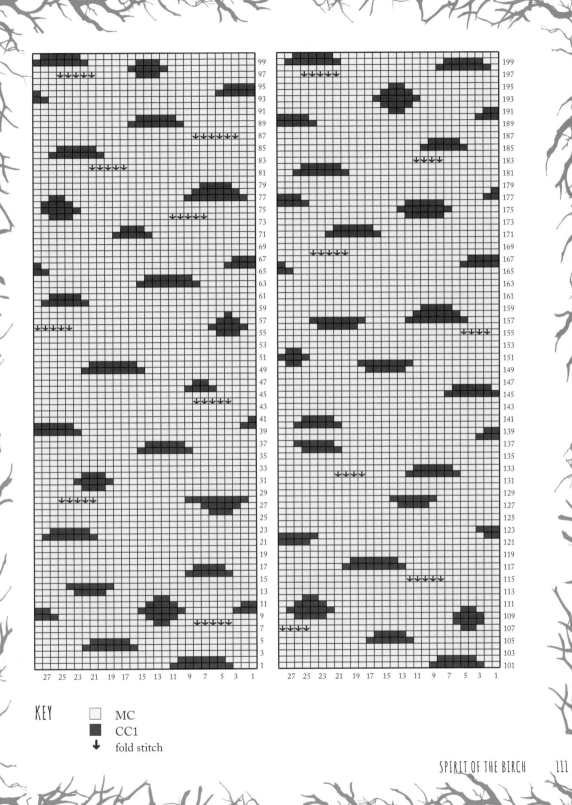

KEY

□ MC

■ CC1

↓ fold stitch

CHART AND COLORWORK NOTES

When working from the chart, knit all stitches, starting on chart row 1. MC is white and CC1 is the brown for the "birch tree knots." The arrow symbol means to make a fold stitch.

Keep a little pair of scissors with you when doing this project. When you need to add CC1, join the new color and knit the (usually 2–8) stitches while dragging the MC along behind as you go. When you need to switch back to MC, cut off CC1 leaving a 4" (10cm) yarn tail and just let it hang inside. You don't have to weave in ends or carry the CC1 for any distance whatsoever. We will deal with the ends later.

If I may say, I love this birch cuff! I wear mine pretty much every day, even in summer. I put a little essential oil blend (like lavender, spearmint, and sage) on a cotton pad and tuck it inside. The fringe represents the spirit of the birch, or the dryad inside. Don't forget to make your fringe extra long and dramatic.

TO MAKE THE BIRCH SCARF

Work as given for Birch Cuff to **.
Cut off strand of CC2 and cont with MC only.
Using MC, and introducing CC1 only where required, work from chart, starting with chart round 1 and ending with chart round 200. Starting again at chart round 1, work from chart until scarf measures 94" (240cm) from cast-on edge or until you have only enough yarn left for the last 3 rounds.
Join in CC2 (holding it double with MC).
Next round: [K7, k2tog] twice, k8, k2tog. *25 sts.*
Next round: Knit.
Bind off, continuing to hold both yarns together.

TO FELT THE CUFF AND SCARF

After binding off, turn the scarf or cuff wrong side out and tug gently on all of the dangling ends of CC1 yarn. This will cinch the edges of each "birch tree knot" and make them look more realistic. Leave your work wrong side out for felting. IMPORTANT: Start felting your work with the wrong side out. Midway through the felting, the many ends of CC1 will start to become more secure and matt together. At the point when they begin to resist cinching when tugged, cut them to ½" (1.5cm) long, turn the cuff/scarf right side out and finish the felting process.

Birch cuff
I prefer to felt the cuff by hand. That way I can monitor the progress and mold and shape along the way. Plus it's just good fun! Drench the cuff in hot water and add a bit of soap. (Try lavender or patchouli scented!) Squeeze the water out. Rub the cuff this way and that vigorously for 15–30 minutes. Just when you think it is never gonna felt, it suddenly will. Magic! Rinse out the soap and shape to your wrist. Wet wool will work almost like clay so mold it how you like it and leave it to dry overnight. After it dries brush the white fuzzy end furiously with a stiff brush to puff it up. *Done!*

Birch scarf

Felting by hand is great, but we are going to need to pop this thing in the washing machine. Place the scarf inside a zippered pillowcase, and wash on short/hot setting with some detergent and a few towels for extra agitation. Check it often and don't forget to trim the ends of CC1 at some point during the process before they get way too matted into the work. When the scarf is almost felted to your desired perfection, take it out and do a bit of molding and shaping by hand. Then, leave it to dry overnight before adding fringe.

TO ADD THE SCARF FRINGE

Cut approximately 60 strands of MC and 20 strands of CC2 in varying lengths 12–24" (30–60cm) long. Attach each strand individually—to do this, fold the strand in half, pull the fold loop through the scarf with a crochet hook, then pull the ends through the loop and tighten. Attach about 40 strands to each end of the scarf. First attach some shorter ones all around the edges, and then attach longer ones about 1" (2.5cm) up the inside of the tube so they hang down from the middle like jellyfish tentacles. Work the felting process like you did for the cuff but just felt them "lightly" so they still have some sway about them.

Now you are ready to put on your "new beginnings" birch scarf and cuff and play with the magical dryads in the forest. Bless you, forest creature!

THE CHANGELING COLLAR

Faeries like to keep their options open. Luckily for them, this little reversible collar can be flipped and worn two different ways. On the flipside, faeries hate to make decisions. Looks like the changeling collar will keep them in front of the mirror all day!

OWL EXPERIENCE LEVEL

SIZES	XS	S	M	L	XL
	12–12½"	13–13½"	14–14½"	15–15½"	16–16½"
	30.5–32cm	33–34.5cm	35.5–37cm	38–39.5cm	40.5–42cm

Note: This collar should be worn very close to the neck almost like a choker. Measure your neck at the smallest part to determine size.

YOU WILL NEED

A fingering-weight yarn (1), such as Knit Picks *Palette* (231yd/211m per ball; 100% Peruvian Highland wool) in each of the following five colors:

* **MC1** 1 × 50g ball in dark green (25543 Larch Heather)
* **MC2** 1 × 50g ball in light green (24006 Verdant Heather)
* **CC1** 1 × 50g ball in light purple (24012 Iris Heather)
* **CC2** 1 × 50g ball in mid purple (24259 Huckleberry Heather)
* **CC3** 1 × 50g ball in antique bronze (25100 Serpentine)

* US size 3 (3.25mm) circular needle, 24" (60cm) long
* US size C/2 (2.75mm) crochet hook
* Small shaft button
* Stitch markers and blunt-ended yarn needle

GAUGE

26 sts and 34 rows to 4" (10cm) square measured over St st using US size 3 (3.25mm) needles and MC1 (or MC2). *Use needles needed to obtain correct gauge.*

TINY OWL STITCH DICTIONARY

See page 9 for general knitting abbreviations.

Ready? Let's go!

TO MAKE THE COLLAR

The two layers (sides) of the collar are made in one piece.

Side 1 of collar (dark green side)

Using US size 3 (3.25mm) circular needle and MC1, cast on 80 (86: 92: 98: 104) sts.

Work back and forth in rows on circular needle as follows:

Row 1 (RS): P27 (29: 31: 33: 35), place marker, p26 (28: 30: 32: 34), place marker, purl to end of row.

Note: Slip markers from left to right needle when they are reached in each row, but ignore them for now.

Beg seed-stitch border as follows:

Row 2 (WS): *K1, p1; rep from *.

Row 3: *P1, k1; rep from *.

Row 4: Rep row 2.

This completes the seed-stitch border.

Beg increases as follows:

Row 5: Inc 1, knit to first marker, slip marker, inc 1, knit to 2 sts before 2nd marker, inc 1, k1, slip marker, knit to last 2 sts, inc 1, k1. *84 (90: 96: 102: 108) sts.*

Row 6: Purl.

[Repeat rows 5 and 6] 12 times more until there are 52 (54: 56: 58: 60) sts between the first and second markers.

Work row 5 once more. *136 (142: 148: 154: 160) sts.*

Next row (WS): Knit (this creates a folding ridge on RS).

Do not bind off, but cut off yarn, leaving a 4" (10cm) yarn tail.

Side 2 of collar (light green side)

With RS facing, join MC2 and work as follows:

Row 1 (RS): Ssk, knit to first marker, slip marker, ssk, knit to 2 sts before next marker, k2tog, slip marker, knit to last 2 sts, k2tog. *132 (138: 144: 150: 156) sts.*

Row 2: Purl.

[Repeat rows 1 and 2] 12 times more until there are 28 (30: 32: 34: 36) sts between the first and second markers.

Work row 1 once more. *80 (86: 92: 98: 104) sts.*

Removing markers on next row, begin seed-stitch border as follows:

Next row (WS): *K1, p1; rep from *.

Next row: *P1, k1; rep from *.

Next row: *K1, p1; rep from *.

Bind off evenly in seed st.

TO EMBROIDER THE FLOWERS

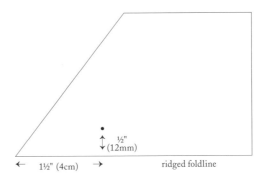

The flowers are embroidered on the points of collar on both sides of the collar—to make it reversible. On each of the four collar points, measure ½" (12mm) from the ridged foldline and 1½" (4cm) in from the side edge—the chart begins here. Place a marker in this stitch to represent closest bottom stitch of the chart. Find and mark the stitch in this way on both sides of the collar and on each of the four points. Now work the embroidery in duplicate stitch on the points of the collar, using the colors noted.

½"
(12mm)

1½" (4cm)

ridged foldline

TO WORK THE CROCHET EDGINGS

The collar is seamed together with single crochet and then a decorative crochet edging is worked along the front edges of the collar.

Fold the collar in half lengthwise with wrong sides together. Hold the folded collar so that Side 2 (the light green side) is facing you and the open edges are at the top and sides. Using crochet hook and MC1 and working through both layers of collar, join yarn with a slip stitch to beginning of open side edge of collar, then work single crochet stitches evenly along first short side edge, along long neck edge of collar and along second short side edge, turn.

Still using MC1 and with Side 1 facing you, work the decorative front crochet edging on the first front edge as follows:

Row 1: Ch 2 (counts as first dc), then working into front loops only, evenly space 27 dc into the sc along front collar edge, turn.

Side 2 is now facing you.

Row 2: Ch 1, 1 sc in first dc, *3 ch, 1 sc in each of next 5 dc; rep from * to end, ch 3, 1 slip stitch in top of 2-ch at end. (The first 3-ch loop you made is the buttonhole.)

Fasten off.

Work along the other front edge as follows:
Using crochet hook and MC1 and with Side 1 facing you, join yarn with a slip stitch to *top* corner of other front edge of collar and work rows 1 and 2 as given for other end. (This time, the 3-ch loop at top is where the button is attached.)

As Side 1 of the collar looks pretty plain compared to Side 2, feel free to work a decorative crochet border along the front neck edges as follows:
Using crochet hook and MC2 and with Side 1 facing you, join yarn with a slip stitch to the bottom right-hand corner point of the *knitting*. Work a slip stitch into each knit stitch of Side 1 only along the front edge, neck edge, and other front edge, ending at the other collar point.

Fasten off.

Sew on button and weave in all yarn ends.

CHART KEY

- MC1
- MC2
- CC1
- CC2
- CC3

CHART A FOR SIDE 1 OF COLLAR

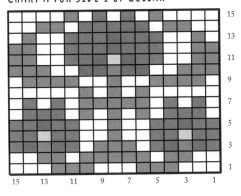

CHART B FOR SIDE 2 OF COLLAR

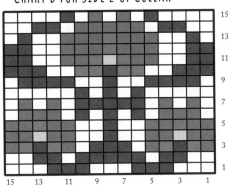

MIDSUMMER NIGHT'S DREAM

Midsummer's Eve is the shortest night of the year and brings out
all sorts of wee faery folk looking for fun. To see them you must
only sit very still and rub a bit of fern seed into your eyes at the
stroke of midnight. Wearing this hood helps, too.

OWL EXPERIENCE LEVEL

SIZE

Two sizes to fit adult and child
Note: The adult size comes first and the child's
size follows in parentheses ( ) where it differs. The
child's size uses only small leaves and moonflowers.

YOU WILL NEED

A medium-weight mohair/wool yarn (4), such as
Classic Elite *La Gran* (106yd/97m per ball;
78.4% mohair, 17.3% wool, 4.3% nylon) in the
following four colors:
* **MC** 2 × 50g balls in gray-brown (6545 Barley),
  for hood—use two strands held together
* **CC1** 1 × 50g ball in green (6539 Eucalyptus
  Green), for leaves and vines
* **CC2** 1 × 50g ball in off-white (6516
  Natural), for moonflowers and white pips
* **CC3** 1 × 50g ball in purple (6538 Raisin),
  for purple pips

* **CC4** 1 × 50g ball of a double-knitting-
  weight wool tweed yarn (3), such as Rowan
  Tweed (129yd/118m per ball; 100% wool) in
  off-white (580 Arncliffe), for antlers
* US size 15 (10mm) circular knitting needle,
  24" (60cm) long
* Pair of US size 15 (10mm) knitting needles
* Pair of US size 9 (5.5mm) knitting needles
* Set of US size 9 (5.5mm) double-pointed
  knitting needles (dpns)
* US sizes F/5 and K/10½ (3.75mm and
  6.5mm) crochet hooks
* Off-white sewing thread, for sewing on antlers
* Stitch markers and blunt-ended yarn needle

GAUGE

9 sts to 4" (10cm) measured over St st using
US size 15 (10mm) needles and MC held double.
Use needle size needed to obtain correct gauge.

Ready? Let's go!

TO MAKE THE HOOD

Using US size 15 (10mm) circular needle and 2 strands of MC held together, cast on 66 (56) sts. Work back and forth in rows on circular needle as follows:

Row 1 (RS): Knit.
Row 2: Purl.
Rows 3 and 4: Rep rows 1 and 2.
Row 5: Ssk, knit to last 2 sts, k2tog.
Row 6: Purl.
[Repeat rows 5 and 6] 4 times more, so ending with a WS row. *56 (46) sts.*
Mark end of last row.
Starting with a knit row, work in St st until hood measures 8"/20cm (7"/18cm) from marker, ending with a RS row.
Do NOT cut off yarn or bind off.

TO GRAFT THE HOOD SEAM

Prepare the hood stitches for grafting the hood seam as follows:
Slip first 28 (23) sts onto one US size 15 (10mm) straight knitting needle and last 28 (23) sts onto another—with both needle points facing away from the center of the hood stitches.
Align the needles, with the wrong sides of the knitting together, and hold both needles in your left hand, points facing right—the working yarn will be coming off the back needle.

Cut off yarn, leaving a *very* long yarn tail for seaming. Thread the long yarn tail onto a blunt-ended yarn needle and graft the edges together using Kitchener stitch as explained on page 31.

TO MAKE THE LARGE LEAVES (MAKE 10)

Using US size 9 (5.5mm) needles and CC1, cast on 3 sts, leaving a 8" (20cm) yarn tail.
Row 1 and all odd-numbered rows: Purl.
Row 2: K1, [yo, k1] twice. *5 sts.*
Row 4: K2, yo, k1, yo, k2. *7 sts.*
Row 6: K3, yo, k1, yo, k3. *9 sts.*
Rows 8 and 10: Knit.
Row 12: Ssk, knit to last 2 sts, k2tog. *7 sts.*
Row 13: Purl.
Rows 14, 15, 16, and 17: [Rep rows 12 and 13] twice. *3 sts.*
Row 18: Slip 1, k2tog, pass slipped st over 2nd st on right needle and off right needle.
Cut off yarn and fasten off. Weave in yarn end.

TO MAKE THE SMALL LEAVES (MAKE 12)

Using US size 9 (5.5mm) needles and CC1, cast on 3 sts, leaving a 8" (20cm) yarn tail.
Row 1 and all odd-numbered rows: Purl.
Row 2: K1, [yo, k1] twice. *5 sts.*
Rows 4 and 6: Knit.
Row 8: Ssk, k1, k2tog. *3 sts.*
Row 10: Slip 1, k2tog, pass slipped st over 2nd st on right needle and off right needle.
Cut off yarn and fasten off. Weave in yarn end.

TO MAKE THE LARGE MOONFLOWERS (MAKE 4)

Using US size 9 (5.5mm) needles and CC2, cast on 7 sts.
Row 1 and all odd-numbered rows: Purl.
Row 2: *K1, m1; rep from * to last st, k1. *13 sts.*
Row 4: *K1, m1; rep from * to last st, k1. *25 sts.*

**Purl 1 row.

Bind off, leaving a long yarn tail.

Using a blunt-ended yarn needle and long yarn tail, seam the strip into a cone.

Stem

To make the moonflower stem, thread a 16" (40cm) strand of CC1 through the base of the flower and leave ends to hang equidistantly to felt later.

TO MAKE THE SMALL MOONFLOWERS (MAKE 5)

Using US size 9 (5.5mm) needles and CC2, cast on 4 sts.

Row 1 and all odd-numbered rows: Purl.

Row 2: *K1, m1; rep from * to last st, k1. *7 sts.*

Row 4: *K1, m1; rep from * to last st, k1. *13 sts.*

Complete as for large flower from **.

TO MAKE THE PIPS (MAKE 18 IN CC3 AND 3 IN CC2)

Using a US size 9 (5.5mm) needles, cast on 2 sts, leaving a 5" (12.5cm) yarn tail.

Row 1: K1, yo, k1. *3 sts.*

Row 2: Purl.

Row 3: Slip 1, k2tog, pass slipped st over 2nd st on right needle and off right needle.

Cut off yarn, leaving a 5" (12.5cm) yarn tail and fasten off.

Tie long yarn tails in a double knot. This will make a little round pip. Leave tails dangling and use to attach to hood later.

TO MAKE THE VINES (MAKE 3)

Using US size K/10½ (6.5mm) crochet hook, crochet a chain 12" (30.5cm) long. Fasten off.

TO MAKE THE CURLY VINES (MAKE 4)

Using US size F/5 (3.75mm) crochet hook, crochet a chain 7" (18cm) long. Fasten off.

TO MAKE THE ANTLERS (MAKE 2)

Using 5.5mm (US size 9) dpns and CC2, work as for antlers for Deer With Little Antlers Hat on page 15, working up to ***.

OK, now felt them!

TO FELT THE DECORATIVE PIECES

Felt the leaves, flowers, pips, vines, and antlers by hand using a gentle felting style, shaping as you go. Drench each piece in hot water and add a bit of soap. Squeeze water out. Felt as follows:

Leaves
Keep them pressed flat into your hands as you felt and shape them by rubbing your hands together.

Flowers
Pinch and form the cone shape as you go and roll the stem wool between your hands to felt/fuse them.

Pips
Gently rub them in a circular motion on your palm for about a minute. They should be lightly felted.

Vines
Roll them between your hands. Let curly vines retain their spirals as you felt them. Don't press too hard.

Antlers
You can be more vigorous with the antlers and don't give up shaping until they are just right.

Rinsing and drying
Rinse out the soap and leave the pieces to dry in the desired shape.

TO DECORATE THE HOOD

If you don't have a hat model for the next part, you can do what I did. Blow up a balloon to the desired size and tape it upright into a vase or cup. Put hood on the balloon while you attach the flora. *Um, be careful with that needle now!*

Antlers
Position the antlers either side of the hood and whipstitch them in place around their bases, using off-white sewing thread.

Tassels

No seams here! You will hand felt a moonflower stem to a leaf stem as they pass through a stitch on the hood.

1. Each side tassel consists of two large moonflowers and one small moonflower, two large leaves and one small leaf.

2. Run a moonflower stem through a stitch at the front corner point of the hood. Now hand felt the stem to a leaf stem on the other side by completely overlapping stems and working the felting process until they fuse into one big stem.

3. Repeat for the remainder of the tassel flora at your whim.

Crown

Using matching yarn and a blunt-ended yarn needle, attach the remaining curly vines, flowers, leaves, and pips in little clusters all around the brim of the hat in a carefree fashion. Put pips in clusters of two or three. Try putting a pip on the end of a curly vine.

Have fun with the arrangement and don't be afraid to re-do it if it starts looking weird like mine did for a spell.

Good luck seeing the faeries!

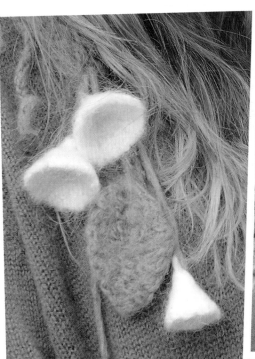

YARN INFORMATION

The yarns used for the designs in this book are listed here. Use the yarn specified when possible. If you use a substitute, choose a yarn in the same weight group (see Standard Yarn Weight System) and with a similar fiber content. Recommended gauge and needle size of the substitute should match the yarn specified. Purchase the correct yarn amount by yardage, not by ball weight.

Berroco *Flicker®*
Worsted-weight alpaca-mix yarn (4); 87% alpaca, 8% acrylic, 5% other fibers; 189yd/173m per 50g hank; 20 sts and 28 rows to 4"/10cm over St st using US 9 (5.5mm) needles; berroco.com

Berroco *Ultra® Alpaca*
Worsted-weight alpaca/wool yarn (4); 50% alpaca, 50% wool; 215yd/198m per 100g hank; 20 sts and 26 rows to 4"/10cm over St st using US 8 (5mm) needles; berroco.com

Blue Sky Alpacas *Melange*
Sport-weight yarn (2), 100% alpaca; 110yd/100m per 50g hank; 20–24 sts to 4"/10cm over St st using US 3–5 (3.25–3.75mm) needles; blueskyalpacas.com

Blue Sky Alpacas *Royal*
Fingering-weight alpaca yarn (1); 100% royal alpaca; 288yd/263m per 100g hank; 24–28 sts to 4"/10cm over St st using US 2–3 (2.75–3.25mm) needles; blueskyalpacas.com

Blue Sky Alpacas *Sport Weight*
Sport-weight yarn (2); same specifications as Blue Sky Alpacas *Melange*; blueskyalpacas.com

Brooklyn Tweed Loft
Fingering-weight wool yarn (1); 100% wool; 275yd/251.5m per 50g hank; 24–32 sts to 4"/10cm over St st using US 0–4 (2–3.5mm) needles; brooklyntweed.net

Cascade *Ecological Wool*
Bulky-weight wool yarn (5); 100% natural Peruvian wool; 478yd/437m per 250g hank; 14–16 sts to 4"/10cm over St st using US 9–10 (5.5–6mm) needles; cascadeyarns.com

Cascade *Pastaza*
Heavy-worsted-weight llama/wool yarn (4); 50% llama, 50% wool; 132yd/120m per 100g hank; 16 sts to 4"/10cm over St st using US 9 (5.5mm) needles; cascadeyarns.com

Classic Elite *La Gran*
Medium-weight mohair/wool yarn (4); 78.4% mohair, 17.3% wool, 4.3% nylon; 106yd/97m per 50g ball; 16 sts to 4"/10cm over St st using US 9 (5.5mm) needles; classiceliteyarns.com

Erika Knight *Fur Wool*
Super-bulky-weight wool-mix fur-effect yarn (6); 97% wool, 3% nylon; 44yd/40m per 100g hank; 5½ sts and 8 rows to 4"/10cm over St st using US 19 (15mm) needles; erikaknight.co.uk

Jamieson's of Shetland *Spindrift*
Fingering-weight wool yarn (1); 100% pure new wool; 115yd/105m per 25g ball; 30 sts and 32 rows to 4"/10cm over St st using US 3 (3.25mm) needles; jamiesonsofshetland.co.uk

Knit Picks *Palette*
Fingering-weight wool yarn (1); 100% Peruvian Highland wool; 231yd/211m per 50g ball; 28–32 sts to 4"/10cm over St st using US 1–3 (2.25–3.25mm) needles; knitpicks.com

Koigu *KPPPM*
Fingering-weight wool yarn (1); 100% merino wool; 170yd/155.5m per 50g hank; 28 sts and 36 rows to 4"/10cm over St st using US 3 (3mm) needles; koigu.com

Malabrigo *Merino Worsted*
Heavy-worsted-weight wool yarn (4); 100% merino wool; 210yd/192m per 100g hank; 18 sts to 4"/10cm over St st using US 7–9 (4.5–5.5mm) needles; malabrigoyarn.com

Manos del Uruguay *Wool Clasica*
Aran-weight wool yarn (4); 100% wool; 138yd/126m per 100g hank; 16 sts to 4"/10cm over St st using US 9 (5.5mm) needles; kyarns.com

Misti Alpaca *Chunky*
Bulky-weight alpaca yarn (5); 100% baby alpaca; 109yd/100m per 100g hank; 14 sts to 4"/10cm over St st using US 10 (6mm) needles; mistialpaca.com

Naturally *Sensation*
Aran-weight angora/wool yarn (4); 70% merino wool, 30% angora; 131yd/120m per 50g hank; 20 sts to 4"/10cm over St st using US 6 (4mm) needles; naturallyyarnsnz.com

Plymouth *Encore Worsted*
Worsted-weight acrylic/wool yarn (4); 75% acrylic, 25%wool; 200yd/183m per 100g ball; 20 sts to 4"/10cm over St st using US 8 (5mm) needles; plymouthyarn.com

Rowan *Alpaca Cotton*
Aran-weight alpaca/cotton yarn (4); 72% alpaca/28% cotton; 148yd/135m per 50g ball; 16 sts and 23 rows to 4"/10cm over St st using US 8 (5mm) needles; knitrowan.co.uk

Rowan *Big Wool*
Super-bulky-weight wool yarn (6); 100% merino wool; 87yd/80m per 100g ball; 7½–9 sts and 10–12½ rows to 4"/10cm over St st using US 15–19 (10–15mm) needles; knitrowan.co.uk

Rowan *Cocoon*
Bulky-weight wool/mohair yarn (5); 80% merino wool, 20% kid mohair; 126yd/115m per 100g ball; 14 sts and 16 rows to 4"/10cm over St st using US 10½ (7mm) needles; knitrowan.co.uk

Rowan *Drift*
Super-bulky-weight wool yarn (6); 100% merinowool; 87yd/80m per 100g ball; 7½–9 sts and 10–12½ rows to 4"/10cm over St st using US 15–19 (10–15mm) needles; knitrowan.co.uk

Rowan *Felted Tweed DK*
Double-knitting-weight wool/ alpaca tweed yarn (3); 50% merino wool, 25% alpaca, 25% viscose; 191yd/175m per 50g ball; 22–24 sts and 30–32 rows to 4"/10cm over St st using US 5–6 (3.75–4mm) needles; knitrowan.co.uk

Rowan *Fine Tweed*
Sport-weight wool tweed yarn (2); 100% wool; 98yd/90m per 25g ball; 26½ sts and 38 rows to 4"/10cm over St st using US 3 (3.25mm) needles; knitrowan.co.uk

Rowan *Kid Classic*
Aran-weight wool/mohair yarn (4); 70% lambswool, 22% kid mohair, 8% nylon; 153yd/140m per 50g ball; 18–19 sts and 23–25 rows to 4"/10cm over St st using US 8–9 (5–5.5mm) needles; knitrowan.co.uk

Rowan *Kidsilk Haze*
Fine-weight mohair/silk yarn (2); 70% super kid mohair, 30% silk; 229yd/210m per 25g ball; 18–25 sts and 23–34 rows to 4"/10cm over St st using US 3–8 (3.25–5mm) needles; knitrowan.co.uk

Rowan *Pure Wool 4-Ply*
Fingering-weight wool yarn (1); 100% superwash wool; 174yd/160m per 50g ball; 28 sts and 38 rows to 4"/10cm over St st using US 6 (4mm) needles; knitrowan.co.uk

Rowan *Tweed*
Double-knitting-weight wool tweed yarn (3); 100% wool; 129yd/118m per 50g ball; 21 sts and 30 rows to 4"/10cm over St st using US 6 (4mm) needles; knitrowan.co.uk

Rowan *Tweed Aran*
Aran-weight wool tweed yarn (4); 100% wool; 105yd/96m per 50g ball; 17–19 sts and 23–25 rows to 4"/10cm over St st using US 7–8 (4.5–5mm) needles; knitrowan.co.uk

Standard Yarn Weight System

Categories of yarn, gauge ranges, and recommended knitting needle sizes from the Craft Yarn Council of America.

Yarn weight symbol and category name	0 Lace	1 Super Fine	2 Fine	3 Light	4 Medium	5 Bulky	6 Super Bulky
Types of yarn in category	lace, fingering, 10-count crochet thread	fingering, sock, baby, UK 4-ply	sport, baby	DK, light worsted	worsted, afghan, aran	chunky, craft, rug	bulky, roving
Knit gauge range to 4"/10cm over St st	33–40 sts	27–32 sts	23–26 sts	21–24 sts	16–20 sts	12–15 sts	6–11 sts
Recommended US needle size	000–1	1–3	3–5	5–7	7–9	9–11	11 and larger
Recommended metric needle size	1.5–2.25mm	2.25–3.25mm	3.25–3.75mm	3.75–4.5mm	4.5–5.5mm	5.5–8mm	8mm and larger

ACKNOWLEDGMENTS

Huge love and thanks to my family and friends for all of your never-ending support. I like your squeals of excitement when I show you new things—it keeps me going! But I also appreciate your "Umm… what is that thing you are making. It's weird…" because it forces me to try again, get better, and challenge myself, or maybe even stick to my guns!

I'd also like to thank every blessed soul that was involved in making this book a reality, especially my woe absorber Lisa Pendreigh. It has been a thrilling journey that I am so grateful for and will never forget.

Last but not least I'd like to thank all of the Owlies of TOKland for your continued excitement and support. You make the common room what it is —a magical healing place of love and joy joy joy!

Thank you all and happy knits!

Love,
Stephanie *xoxo*
Tiny Owl Knits

Q. JUST WHAT IN TARNATION ARE THE OWLIES OF TOKLAND?

A. Good question! Come join in the Owlie fun here: www.ravelry.com/groups/tiny-owl-knits. We have a blast!

For more information and patterns from Tiny Owl Knits, please go to www.tinyowlknits.com